YOUNG WAYFARERS
OF THE EARLY WEST

YOUNG WAYFARERS
OF THE EARLY WEST

BY OLIVE W. BURT

ILLUSTRATED BY JULES GOTLIEB

HAWTHORN BOOKS, INC.
PUBLISHERS NEW YORK CITY

YOUNG WAYFARERS OF THE EARLY WEST

FOR

LISA DUNCAN

A teen-ager I am proud to call my friend

Tokyo

CONTENTS

YOUNG WAYFARERS
OF THE EARLY WEST

INTRODUCTION

Teen-agers played an important role in the development of the American West. Every family chronicle mentions young boys and girls who, traveling across plains and mountains and deserts, assumed the stature of adults. Boys of twelve and thirteen became men on the long and difficult journey. Little girls worked alongside their mothers, took care of younger children, cooked and sewed, tended chickens and milked cows with all the assurance of an older hand.

Along the old Oregon Trail, across the plains, mountains and deserts with the fleeing Mormon Saints, around the Horn or across the Isthmus of Panama with their gold-hungry parents, boys and girls made their way heroically, unquestioningly, taking hardships and labor as a matter of course. There may have been deserters along the way, but if so they have left nothing by which to remember them.

These were young people traveling with their parents, brothers, sisters and friends in a sort of moving community. But there were others who went West on their own, without the support and protection of their relatives. Others had to

11

leave the security of their families and take jobs with strangers in order to earn money to help those left behind. This happened most often when the father had died and the widowed mother found it difficult to support her children.

Such independent and responsible youngsters often contributed as much as any man in the movements and activities that were building up the cities of the West. In history and legend they are often mentioned in a casual way. A sentence here, a paragraph there discloses that Jim Bridger was a youth when he joined General William Henry Ashley's band of hard-bitten trappers; that Lorenzo Oatman was but fifteen when he was orphaned by the massacre of most of his family on the Yuma trail.

And there were less heroic young people who made their special contributions to the life and the development of the early West. Seven-year-old Johnny Brier proved to be a hero during the family's crossing of Death Valley in 1849. John M. Browning was making guns in Utah before he was twenty. Mike Fink was an official hunter for the frontier villages when he was seventeen. At sixteen, John Allen Hosmer wrote and published the first book to come from Montana Territory. Sam Houston left home to join the Cherokees when he was sixteen. Otto Mears was an itinerant peddler before he reached his teens. He made a regular business of supplying the gold-mining camps of the Mother Lode in California with needed supplies.

How did these boys come to be where they were? How did they react to the situation? What had their lives been like? Had anything prepared them to meet their new life? Did they live to make a worth-while contribution to the new region?

Any reader of Western history will be aware that there were other teen-agers who chose not to build, but to destroy. Many of the "bad men" of the early West began their careers in crime before they were twenty. They left their stories, to be retold again and again in legend and ballad. But that is all they left. The young people who contributed something worth while are those who took part in the great movements westward; who met the challenges of hardship and danger with true courage and responsibility.

It is to pay tribute to these heroic young people that this book has been written.

CHAPTER ONE

A CITY IS BORN
René Auguste Chouteau (1749–1829)
and the Founding of St. Louis

The boy, sitting in the small boat, was excited. His brown eyes roved from side to side, studying the riverbanks that rose steeply from the water. He had forgotten the tall man beside him; had forgotten the voyageurs, or boatmen, whose naked backs gleamed with sweat as they poled the small craft against the current. He had forgotten the French soldiers at Fort Chartres where, for three long months, he and his companion had lived and where they had deposited, for safe-keeping, bales and boxes of trade goods. He had even forgotten his mother and his five-year-old brother who had been left behind at the busy little village of Ste. Genevieve.

All these things were in the past, as was his thirteenth birthday celebrated by a little "fete" at one of their night camps on the river last August. This was a new time—a new experience.

The boy's bright, intelligent face set him apart from the voyageurs as clearly as did his clothing. His leather trousers and shirt, though tough and serviceable, were so finely tailored and of such excellent skins, and were worn with such an air, that one knew at once that this was no common youth, but a gentleman born and used to elegant surroundings. The tradition he had left behind seemed only to increase his interest in this new environment.

Since the party had left Fort Chartres, they had been traveling in unknown country. Enormous trees that had never felt the bite of an ax blade towered above the river. Those on the west sent long shadows across the stream. Indians or wild animals might be lurking there, watching them.

"Observe with care, *mon cher*," the tall man said in French. "Somewhere we shall find it, the spot exactly right for our new post."

It was a needless admonition, for Auguste Chouteau's

15

eyes were always observant. It was this alertness, this eager attention that had endeared the boy to his companion, Pierre Ligueste de Laclede, and had earned him the right to accompany the man on this expedition into the wilderness of the Mississippi River country beyond the last known settlement.

"It is not here," the boy said quietly. "The banks here rise too steeply. It would be difficult even for Indian canoes to find harbor."

Some authorities say Laclede was the boy's stepfather; others do not try to unravel the problem. Auguste's mother, however, is generally referred to as Madame Chouteau. The records say nothing of the boy's father. All that is known is that in July of 1763, Ligueste de Laclede and his partner

in the New Orleans firm of Maxent, Laclede & Co. had been granted the exclusive right to trade for furs with the Indians along the Mississippi above Fort Chartres by the French Government.

The partners acted immediately. On August 3, Laclede had set out with a party of thirty men and the boy to establish a trading post from which to carry on this business. It is thought that Auguste's mother, with a younger son, had accompanied the party but had been left at Ste. Genevieve, which was already a thriving village on the west bank of the river.

Further up the river, on the eastern bank, was Fort Chartres, a French outpost. All this region had been under French control, but now rumors that it had been given away by King Louis XV had been confirmed. The lands to the west had been ceded to Spain; those on the eastern bank of the river, to England. All during the past months the party had waited at Fort Chartres for word that they could proceed with their plans.

Now it was December, and they were on their way upriver. As yet there were neither French nor Spanish nor English here to contest their right. If they were wise and careful, they could reap a fortune in furs before they were challenged.

Toward sundown, Laclede gave an exclamation of delight. He pointed to the western bank of the river and the boy's eyes lit up as they followed the man's gesture. There, just ahead of the pirogue, was a small, natural harbor with the bank rising in shallow shelves toward the wooded bluff above.

"*C'est bon!*" Auguste cried. "It is right, sir! It is perfect!"

Laclede gave a sharp command and the voyageurs brought the small craft to the sandy shore. Laclede leaped out, with Auguste at his heels. They gazed with delight on the scene before them.

Directly below was the broad river, flowing rather quietly here. To the north lay a wide, lush plain rich in trees and grass, sparkling with streams flowing toward the river. To

18

the south, the land sloped gently upward to the wooded summit.

"This is the place for the outpost!" Laclede cried. "Here can rise one of the greatest cities of the continent. And yet, we must make certain. We shall continue up the river, but I know we cannot find a better site."

Their journey upstream yielded one pleasant surprise. On the second day, they came to the mouth of the Missouri River and saw the waters of that mighty river pouring into the one they were following. This convinced them that they needed to go no farther. The site they had discovered below could not be bettered. Indian canoes coming down the Missouri from the fur-rich country to the northwest would have but a few miles to travel down the Mississippi to the post. At the same time, it would be right in the path of those moving either up or down the great river. Laclede and Auguste agreed that the thing to do now was to return to Fort Chartres and send word to New Orleans that the site had been selected, and work on the post would begin in the spring.

In February of 1764, Laclede was ready to begin erecting buildings for the new post. He did not accompany his men to the site, however. Instead, he sent young Auguste Chouteau, not yet fourteen years old, as commander of a group of thirty workmen. Auguste was to proceed to the site they had selected and there supervise the construction of the post.

The boy apparently accepted the responsibility without any qualms. He knew that trees must be felled, streets laid out, cabins built and the Indians conciliated. This was a big undertaking for a youth, but it seems that no one had any doubts that the boy was equal to the task.

On February 15, 1764, Auguste landed with his party on the west bank of the Mississippi. He made camp that night in a grove of walnut trees at the foot of what one day would become Walnut Street. At dawn the next morning, a trumpet sounded and work began.

The first task was to lay out the streets. At the head of his crew, the youth strode along the river bank, pointing out where the first street should lie. He named this street the Rue Royale. Further up the slope he marked out another street, Rue de L'Eglise—the street of the Church. Auguste was a devout Catholic and felt that a church was one of the first buildings that should be erected in any community. Still further from the river and paralleling the other two streets, he planned the Rue des Granges—the street of the Barns.

Intersecting these streets, running from the river up the slope, the boy designated the Rue Bonhomme and the Rue de la Tour.

With his main streets determined, Auguste pointed out the sites where he wanted the church, Laclede's house and his own home built. A storehouse and watchtower were also necessary, and Auguste selected sites for these buildings.

He set his men to work. They felled the walnut trees and stripped off the branches. The logs were set close together, upright in the ground, to form strong walls. The roofs were thatched with prairie grass. A firehole was dug in the center of the floor and a smokehole left above it in the roof. Later, stone fireplaces and chimneys would replace this primitive arrangement, but the boy knew that haste was necessary if they were to establish their post before anyone decided to interfere.

He and Laclede had already decided on a name for their settlement. They would call it St. Louis. Those who wished to could consider that it was named for Louis IX, the Crusader King. At the same time it would do honor to the present monarch, Louis XV.

Things were well under way when Laclede came upriver to check the camp's progress. He was so well satisfied that he did not stay long, but set off into the wilderness to start buying furs from the Indians. Such activity was more agreeable to his roving nature than any other life. He could not bear being confined to the management of a post.

Laclede had scarcely left when the Missouri Indians of the region decided to show their friendliness by moving into the camp. They rolled up their skin wigwams, packed their robes and utensils, gathered their dogs and children and came. Too close for the comfort of the Frenchmen, they set up their wigwams beside the rising cabins.

Auguste sent a messenger to find Laclede and tell him what was happening. But he could not wait for help from Laclede. The Indians were friendly enough, but they disrupted the work of the camp. The braves loafed about under the trees, watching the workmen. They appropriated anything left lying about, either by stealth or openly, under the very eyes of the Frenchmen.

Auguste saw that he would have to assume authority immediately, or he would be helpless. Donning his best outfit, powdering his hair and trying to seem dignified, he strode across the grass to the most pretentious of the wigwams. The owner, a tall, imposing Missouri, came out to meet his guest.

Auguste, of course, could neither speak nor understand the language of the Indians. He was wholly unacquainted with the sign language which would later serve so many white men in their dealings with the native Americans. But there are certain friendly gestures, certain agreeable tones of voice, certain facial expressions which cannot be mistaken. Young Auguste had to rely on these in communicating with the invaders.

He managed to make the Missouri chieftain understand that he wished to have a powwow with the men of the tribe. The meeting was called immediately, and the boy stood before the assembly with all the authority of fine clothing and an assured bearing. Fortunately, he soon discovered a nondescript fellow who had somehow acquired a little French and who could act as a makeshift interpreter. With this meager help, Auguste made the Indians understand that he accepted their neighborliness with genuine gratitude. The Missouri Indians also evinced only goodwill.

22

"We can live together in harmony," the boy said carefully in French, hoping his tone would convey his sincerity. "But you must obey the rules I have laid down for my workmen. No one is permitted to be idle. There is much to be done." He gestured toward the empty square where he planned to build his own home—the Chouteau House, the first real house in the settlement. He had already decided that Laclede would not often be on hand and that he, Auguste, must assume the responsibility of managing the post. He intended to support this responsibility by having an imposing residence. Now he continued, "If you remain among us, you must provide your own food and you must assist us with our work. You, too, will benefit from what we do here."

With difficulty, but with patience, persuasiveness and the meager help of the interpreter, Auguste went on to explain that his men were building a great mansion which would add to the glory of the Missouri nation as well as to the honor of the white man. This great house would stand in the center of the village and would protect them all. No hostile tribe could breach the walls. Also, much food would be stored therein. When bad times came and game was scarce, all could come here and obtain food.

The Indians listened politely and grunted. Auguste could not tell how well his message had been received, but he continued as if confident of acceptance. "In order to share the benefits of this great mansion, all must share in the labor of building it. Now," he turned to the head man of his crew, "Now, Jean, give each of these men a shovel or pick or ax and set them all to work excavating for the mansion, as I have drawn up the plans for the foundation."

With that, the boy strode away from the council, head up, shoulders squared. He hoped he looked important enough to impress his visitors. They must work or they would be an unbearable burden.

The Indians watched him go. There were tolerant grins on the dark faces, but they made no move to obey the youth's command. Jean, however, with a couple of workmen, went to the storehouse and brought back picks, shovels and broad-bladed spades. These he distributed to the Indians. Then, as they sat watching, he began to dig a trench along the line marked out by Auguste. The Indians nodded. They understood what he wanted.

As at a signal, they rose from their lounging positions and departed, their tools clutched in their hands. In dismay, Jean watched them go. Now, he thought, the Frenchmen had lost not only the stolen objects, but these tools they had so recklessly given into the hands of their visitors. He rushed to the cabin where Auguste was discarding his finery for more appropriate work clothes. When he told what had happened, Auguste dressed quickly and followed his workman out to the square.

There he stopped in amazement. A score of Indian women were wielding pick and shovel with the greatest energy.

Laclede finally returned to find the trenches dug for the foundation of Chouteau House and the stone walls going up. Another substantial house was being erected for him to occupy. He shook his head in amazement.

24

"Why did you call me back, *mon fils?*" he asked. "You do so very well! It is in your blood, *n'est-ce pas?* You have the way. I? I am able to trade beads and trinkets for peltries, but I am no builder of houses. I am no manager of men. Continue, *mon fils,* as you are doing." Then he frowned. "These Indians, they, perhaps, take over the post? Perhaps they should go away, *non?*"

"But, sir!" Auguste protested, "to send them away will only anger them, make them enemies. We cannot afford that."

"*Oui.* I understand!" he grinned suddenly. "I think now I have the solution."

Then he called a meeting of the Missouri braves. In his travels he had acquired a smattering of their language and he felt he could make himself understood. Feigning excitement and terror, he informed the Indians that the British had engaged the Illinois tribes to attack the new post.

"The British, as you understand, hate us French. They plan to murder us all and destroy this post. We are friends, and so I tell you this that you may escape and save yourselves."

Auguste watched the faces of the listeners. His own natural honesty balked at this sort of trick, but Laclede was the boss. And the boy had to admit that perhaps the man was right. At any rate, the Indians lost no time in packing up their wigwams and leaving.

As soon as Auguste's fine house was ready, Laclede went down to Ste. Genevieve and brought back Madame Chouteau and little Pierre. She was there to help her son, now virtually the commander of the post, celebrate his fourteenth birthday. Laclede, always away either to New Orleans or off in the wilderness buying furs, paid scant attention to the affairs of the post. Young Auguste managed everything. He kept the books, maintained friendly relations with the Indians and with the travelers now moving up and down the river in ever increasing numbers. He purchased peltries from the red hunter and white trapper with equal honesty and fairness. His name was respected throughout the region.

During the following summer the British troops took over Fort Chartres, ceded to them by King Louis XV. There was nothing for the dour French commander, Capt. St. Ange de Bellerive, to do but turn over the fort to the British. Unwilling to leave the region he loved, he moved across the river and upstream to St. Louis. This land had been ceded to Spain, but the old French officer felt he would rather be under Spanish rule than British.

With a commissioned French officer in the settlement, the prestige of young Auguste gave way. Captain de Bellerive became commandant of the post, but the boy continued in charge of the affairs of the New Orleans firm of Maxent, Laclede & Co. Other Frenchmen from the eastern bank of the river, unhappy under the British, followed the old Captain and the settlement at St. Louis grew. The French, who had a special knack for trading with the Indians, still enjoyed a monopoly of the fur trade with the twenty-eight principal Indian nations of that region. Captain de Bellerive continued as commandant and Auguste as virtual manager of the post until the arrival of the Spanish officers five years later.

26

By this time, Auguste was out of his teens, having turned twenty on August 14, 1770. His reputation and his fortune were on solid ground. During the six and a half years since he had laid out the first street along the river bank, he had been honest, industrious and thrifty. He had also been generous and hospitable. At twenty, Auguste Chouteau was rich, respected, handsome and prominent in the affairs of his settlement.

The youth, Auguste, was recognized from the very beginning as a leader in the settlement. When Laclede was absent, as he was for long periods at a time, the whole burden of the post fell upon the boy. He handled money and peltries, made decisions and in every way took a man's part in developing the outpost into the great city it became.

Auguste had laid out St. Louis as an outpost for the fur trade. Later, when John Jacob Astor moved his operations to this city, Auguste became a partner with this German immigrant, whose name came to be almost synonymous with the American fur trade. In this capacity he went afield as Laclede had done, visiting the Osage Indians or riding horseback to New York City to consult with Astor. Such a trip to the East Coast required forty days of hard riding. Once there, Auguste would arrange for the shipment of peltries from the northwest to Europe by way of New Orleans.

This city of his birth was always dear to Auguste Chouteau. He visited it whenever he could.

In 1803, through the Louisiana Purchase, the United States acquired the land west of the Mississippi, which had been under Spanish control until ceded to France in 1800.

Now Auguste, who had lived under both French and Spanish rule, became an American citizen. His new government was not slow to honor him. He was appointed a colonel of militia, a Revolutionary War pension agent and Commissioner to deal with the Osage Indians. Due to Auguste's great influence with the Indians, the hostile tribes came to Portage des Sioux, not far from St. Louis, to sign a treaty of peace with the United States. This historic meeting was held in November of 1804.

In 1809, when St. Louis became a city, Auguste Chouteau was named a trustee. The Territorial Legislature of Missouri made him a commissioner to regulate the schools. He was a justice of the peace, a court judge and a bank president.

When he was thirty-six, Auguste married Marie Therese Cerre, the daughter of a merchant in Kaskaskia, Illinois. They had seven children, Auguste, Gabriel, Henri, Edourd, Eulalie, Louise and Emilie. None of these children made remarkable careers in the fur trade, but other Chouteau names were prominent in that business. Pierre, Auguste's younger brother, and his son, Pierre, Jr., were among the most illustrious.

Auguste Chouteau died on February 24, 1829, in his seventy-ninth year. He is buried in Calvary cemetery, St. Louis, on a hill overlooking the great river which he loved so well. On a simple tablet are engraved the words:

"Sa vie a ete de vertus civiles et Sociales." ("His life was of true civility and sociality.")

28

CHAPTER TWO

MOCCASINS WEST
Sacajawea (1790?–1884) and the
Expedition to the Northwest

"This is the happiest day of my life!"

The exclamation burst from the lips of the usually silent Captain Meriwether Lewis. He had never before felt such a surge of exultation and joy. His eyes traveled over the milling crowd—his companions of the past months, their faces aglow with excitement. The Indians were in their bright blankets, and below, on the river, were two sturdy pirogues, made from hollowed out logs, and a half-dozen canoes, already being filled with the jostling, shouting men.

His companion, the red-haired Captain William Clark, laughed aloud. "We've waited for this day! But now— we're off!" And he bounded away toward the waiting vessels. Full of exuberant spirits, he could not wait to act decorously. He leaped into the first pirogue, waved his hand to his watching friend and gave the command, "Pull away!"

The oarsmen bent to their task and the pirogue shot out into midstream.

Above them, on the bank, Captain Lewis turned, his face uplifted toward the West. He would walk to the Mandan village a few miles further upstream, where the party in the boats would camp for the night. A number of the Indians broke away from the crowd still watching the small vessels. They joined the white captain, straggling behind him as he strode along the grassy shore.

It was a bright, sunny afternoon—April 7, 1805, a lovely and auspicious day for the start of their historic journey into the unknown lands of the far Northwest. In his pirogue, Captain Clark chuckled with happiness as he surveyed his companions: the oarsmen, the bearded interpreters Toussaint Charbonneau and George Drewyer, and finally, the Indian girl. Captain Clark's eyes rested on this quiet figure and on the downy black head of the baby just visible in his net basket on his mother's back. The officer nodded with satisfaction.

She seemed to be the calmest and most assured of the entire

party as she sat there, small and slender in her buckskin dress. And yet the dark eyes were watching everything with a bright alertness that belied her tranquil expression. Sacajawea, the Bird Woman. Yes, the Captain told himself, they had done well to employ her. He was sure that she would be invaluable when it came to dealing with the Snake Indians, her people. And she would be no burden, no hindrance to the expedition, even with her baby to care for.

The captain's thoughts went back to the day when he had first seen the young wife of Charbonneau. It had been just a few weeks before her baby was born. Her husband had brought her into the Fort, explaining that she was a Snake and would like to accompany the expedition, which was planning to pass through Snake territory.

At first there had been hesitation about including a woman in the party. Charbonneau's explanation of how his wife had been stolen as a child by a Minnetaree warrior, of how he had purchased her for his wife, of how unhappy she was and lonely for her own people had not swayed the two captains. But the girl's own quiet behavior as she went about her duties in the Indian camp and her courage during the difficult birth of her baby had convinced the officers that it would be worth while to take her along.

"She's scarcely more than a child," Captain Lewis had pointed out. "She can't be more than fifteen or sixteen now, so she was probably very young when she was stolen. Perhaps she can't remember much about her childhood. Perhaps she won't be of much value as a guide. But Charbonneau in-

31

sists that she does recall the language of her people, which neither he nor Drewyer understands, and we do expect to buy horses of the Snakes when we get to their territory. So she may be of some assistance as an interpreter."

Captain Clark had not needed convincing. He, too, had watched the girl about the camp and he felt sure that she would be a real asset to the party. Although her baby was not yet two months old, Captain Clark was glad the Indian girl and her baby had been brought along.

It was a serious and dangerous journey they had undertaken. Nearly two years earlier this vast, unknown territory had been obtained from France, and President Thomas Jefferson wanted to find out just what he had purchased. So he had commissioned the two young officers, Meriwether Lewis and William Clark, to explore the new domain. They were to proceed to the sources of the Missouri River and, if possible, travel all the way to the Pacific coast. They would have to cross lands occupied by various Indian tribes, whose reaction toward invading white men could not be foretold.

With a group of soldiers, boatmen and interpreters, the two officers had left St. Louis in May of 1804. They had reached the Mandan villages on the Missouri, in what is now North Dakota, toward the end of October and decided to winter there. They had constructed Fort Mandan and put in the long, cold months preparing for their journey by learning what they could from the Indians, purchasing food and making clothing. They had been treated well by the Mandans, who had freely told the travelers all they knew about the regions further on.

Captain Clark's eyes had come to rest on Charbonneau, the French-Canadian interpreter they had hired at the Fort. He was a surly, black-browed, black-bearded fellow, strong as an ox. Captain Clark's sunny, happy disposition recoiled from the Frenchman's moodiness. But he tolerated the fellow because of his knowledge of the region, and because of his girl-wife and their baby.

They were in the leading pirogue with the Captain. Here, too, were the indispensable instruments, medicines and papers. Behind this vessel came another pirogue and a half-dozen canoes bearing the rest of the company, tents, food and clothing. They were not going very far this first day, but would camp at the Mandan village. They arrived there by sundown, and a little later Captain Lewis arrived. The Mandan chieftains joined them, and there, beside the river, the travelers spent their last evening among friends.

There was little for Sacajawea to do that first evening, but, when the expedition camped the second night, she picked up a pointed stick and, with her baby on her back, strolled away from the party. She returned an hour later with a basket full of wild artichokes, which she laid before the two captains. They were surprised and delighted. Green vegetables of any kind had been very scarce, and, though these were rather withered and dry, they looked good to the hungry men.

From that time on, the captains grew to expect some such treat from the Indian girl. She had the knack of being able to find the stores of wild vegetables, acorns and nuts which gophers and mice had collected and hidden away for food during the winter. What she contributed in this way to their food supply meant a great deal to the white men.

But Sacajawea took upon her shoulders other tasks to serve the two captains. She washed and repaired their clothing and helped with preparing meals, making camp and loading supplies onto the vessels. No traveling was done at night, so the unloading and reloading were daily chores that had to be done as quickly as possible in order to save time. While many of the men could not swim and were desperately afraid of drowning, the Indian girl had no fear of the water and could swim like an otter. Her skill often came in handy.

On one occasion in mid-May, a sudden squall tipped the "white" pirogue over on its side. It happened that both captains were walking along the shore, and Charbonneau was steersman at the time. Inexperienced as he was at this work, and terrified of the waves whipped high by the wind, the Frenchman let go of the rudder and began to pray hysterically.

The white pirogue was the one in which the officers rode. It also held most of the essential supplies. Now the vessel lay on its side, buffeted by the waves, but saved from total capsize by the sails. Two other men besides Charbonneau were in the craft, but they were clinging to whatever they could find and yelling for help.

On shore, Captain Lewis stripped off his hunting shirt, thinking to go to the rescue. Captain Clark held him back from the impossible task. The only calm person was Sacajawea. She had been sitting in the stern when the vessel tipped over. With her baby on her back as usual, she leaped into the swirling waters and began to retrieve books and papers, packages wrapped in oiled silk and instruments floating away in their cases. As she caught hold of an object, she flung it ashore and reached for the next.

By this time the canoes had come up, the pirogue was righted and brought to shore, where everyone huddled, trying to estimate the damage. The next day, under a bright sun, the soaked articles were dried out and repacked. Sacajawea had saved practically everything of value.

This one act alone, regardless of her other services, was enough to make the Indian girl indispensable. If the instruments, books, notes, medicines and trade goods had been lost, the expedition would have been so seriously handicapped that it might have had to be abandoned far short of the success it finally achieved. The two captains recognized this and, to honor the girl's deed, they named the next river they discovered "Sah-ca-ger-we-ah, or Bird Woman's River." Unfortunately, the stream did not keep this name; today it is known as Crooked Creek in north-central Montana.

Continuing up the Missouri, the party was now coming into the mountains. This country seemed more familiar to the Indian girl. She began to recall with remarkable accuracy scenes and events of her childhood.

So far the explorers had seen buffalo, bears, elk, big horn sheep, beavers, snakes and wild birds. They had come across abandoned Indian camps but they had not yet seen any Indians.

On May 29, they came upon the remains of two large camps which appeared to have been abandoned very recently. Captain Lewis counted the remains of 126 campfires. He called Sacajawea and asked if they had reached the land of the Snake Indians. Charbonneau interpreted for his wife. She poked among the ashes and found the remains of some moccasins. She examined these closely and shook her head.

"No," she told Charbonneau, "these are not the moccasins of my people. I have not seen such before, but I think they belong to some of the people who live on this side of the mountain."

"That would probably be the Atsina," Charbonneau told the two captains. "They are friends of the Blackfeet."

Captain Clark thanked the girl and tossed the rotting moccasins aside. To his companion he said, "See? It is reassuring to have someone who can interpret what we find."

But the weather was not always good, and sometimes the men slogged through mud all day, pulling the vessels against the swift current of a mountain stream. Toothache, tumors, fever and rheumatism attacked the men. They were dosed, even the two leaders, with hot herb tea, salts and bloodletting.

In June, Sacajawea, who had got along very well up to this time, joined the ranks of the ailing. For three days she suffered great pain. The two leaders were worried. They decided that she had caught cold from being in the water, helping with the canoes. Captain Clark decided to "let blood," but it seemed to do the Bird Woman no good.

In spite of all the suffering among the members of the expedition, the group struggled on up the river, now so narrow and rocky that the stream had to be waded while the men dragged the boats upward. Sacajawea took her part in this strenuous work. She had an added handicap, her baby always strapped in his net basket on her back. She was weak and sick, but she did not complain. Captain Clark took time to make bark tea for her and to apply hot poultices to her aching body.

Captain Clark described this part of their journey: "The current is excessively rapid and difficult to ascend. Great numbers of dangerous places, and the fatigue which we have to encounter is incredible. The men in the water from morning till night, hauling the cord and boats, walking on sharp rocks and round, slippery stones which alternately cut their feet and throw them down. Notwithstanding all the difficulty, they go with great cheerfulness." Sacajawea, with her baby on her back, went with them, as long as she could stand. At last, Captain Clark had her placed in a pirogue, with an awning over her to keep off the sun and the rain.

For nearly a week the Bird Woman suffered. Nothing the two leaders could think of gave her any relief. Then Captain Lewis obtained some water from a sulphur spring they passed. He heated this and had her drink it. It helped. A day or two later she had recovered.

Everyone rejoiced. Her willingness to help with any task, and her fortitude under pain and discomfort had won the respect and admiration of those toughened adventures. But she was to give them all another scare a few days later. Charbonneau brought her some green apples and some dried fish. She was hungry after her illness, ate heartily and became very ill. Captain Lewis was angry at the interpreter and gave him a sound scolding.

This spell of sickness was soon over, and Sacajawea was able to walk along the river bank with her husband, Captain Clark and his Negro servant, York. The little party was making its way up a narrow ravine when a sudden cloud-burst sent rain pouring down. The river began to rise with terrifying rapidity. It threatened to fill the narrow channel from side to side, drowning the four walkers. They could not see any way of escape.

Then Captain Clark saw a small ledge above them. He yelled at York, and the servant clambered to safety. Char-

bonneau clawed at the brush, trying to pull himself up. Sacajawea, with Baptiste on her back, was trying to scramble up the muddy slope. The officer slid back, got behind the girl and pushed her and the baby ahead of him to the safety of the narrow ledge.

He was just in time. The water was already lapping around the man's waist. He had lost some of his equipment, but he still clung to his gun. Charbonneau had lost all he carried— gun, shot pouch, horn and tomahawk. And poor little Baptiste was wet and cold and naked. His net cradle-basket, with all his clothes, had been swept away. Shivering, wet and scared, the small party managed to climb out of the ravine. When they looked back down, the churning water was some fifteen feet deep. They wasted no time, but hurried back to the camp where dry clothes, a warm fire and a hot drink revived their spirits.

At the Great Falls of the Missouri the expedition had to leave the river and portage, or carry, their vessels and supplies around the Falls, so they could again use the river beyond the dangerous cataract. The ground here sloped gently upward, but it was covered with cactuses and sharp stones. Moccasins were torn to shreds, feet cut and backs wearied with the burden of carrying heavy supplies. It took more than three weeks to get around the Falls, and everyone rejoiced when the task was done.

Two weeks later they came to a beautiful valley where three rivers met to form the Missouri. While the leaders were deciding to name the streams Jefferson, Madison and Gallatin, Sacajawea was staring enraptured at the surrounding hills. Captain Clark saw her absorption and asked, "What is it?"

Sacajawea began to talk, her voice quivering with emotion. Her husband was called to interpret what she was saying. He listened a moment and then began to talk excitedly.

"She say, Monsieur le Capitaine, this is the place, this meadow, where her people were encamped when Minnetarees they come!"

Now Captain Lewis came to listen while Sacajawea, through Charbonneau, explained that when her people saw the Minnetarees they fled up the river. But the invaders attacked those that lagged. They killed some boys and took

40

women and girls prisoner. Sacajawea and her girl companion had been carried away. She remembered it all.

The party had reached the land of the Snakes. Soon they could abandon their vessels, purchase horses and proceed toward the Pacific. Captain Lewis, impatient to contact Sacajawea's people, set out with Charbonneau and a couple of others to cut across the hills. Captain Clark and the Bird Woman stayed with the canoes. But Captain Lewis found no Indians and, in a few days, he rejoined the main party. He was disappointed that the Indian girl, also, had seen no signs of her people.

Then, on August 8, Sacajawea stopped with a cry of joy. Charbonneau told the leaders that his wife said that the summer home of her people was just over the next mountain. She had recognized the mountain as one her people called Beaver Head, because of its resemblance to that animal. Captain Lewis decided to push ahead again. Sacajawea gave him some advice on how to act when he met the Snakes.

As soon as he caught sight of them, she said, he should take hold of two corners of his blanket, fling it higher than his head and then make a motion as if he were spreading it on the ground. This gesture, repeated three times, would indicate friendship, as it was the movement made when a blanket was spread for a friend. When he came within speaking distance he should shout, *"Tab-ba-bone!"* (white man). Another useful phrase was *"Ah-hi-i."* (I am pleased). Armed with these suggestions and accompanied by George Drewyer, who

41

was adept in the Indian sign language, the captain departed.

Sacajawea and her husband remained with Captain Clark and the main party. They advanced slowly, with the Bird Woman always watching for familiar sights. On the morning of August 17, she was rewarded when she spied a small company of Indians approaching. She began to utter cries of joy, to dance and to whirl about. She put her fingers in her mouth and sucked on them to indicate that the newcomers were of her people.

By now, Captain Clark had discovered Drewyer among the advancing Indians. Drewyer explained that Captain Lewis was just ahead. He had found the Indians and had made friends with them. The sudden realization of their hopes sent every member of the expedition into wild excitement. They shouted and danced. Sacajawea and Captain Clark joined the Indians and started off across the hills.

As they neared the camp, one young woman left the waiting group and came running toward Sacajawea. She stopped in front of Bird Woman, stared a minute and then, with a cry of joy, flung her arms about the girl. Sacajawea, weeping, returned the embrace. The onlookers did not have to be told that this was the very woman who, as a girl, had been stolen away with Sacajawea. Later they learned how she had escaped and found her way back to her people.

Captain Clark went on to where Captain Lewis was standing with a richly robed chieftain. There were salutations, introductions and embraces. Captain Clark was seated upon a white robe, and small shells were braided into his hair. The shells delighted the explorer who knew they must have come from the ocean. He knew then that they were on the western slope of the Continental Divide. All the men removed their moccasins as a sign of peace; the pipe was smoked and passed from hand to hand. Then it was time to powwow, and Captain Clark sent for Sacajawea.

She left the chattering women and came shyly into the council. She kept her head lowered modestly, knowing that it was not customary for a woman to attend a meeting of men. Captain Clark spoke to Charbonneau, who interpreted for his wife. Now she was ready to put the Captain's words into her native tongue. She raised her eyes and looked toward the Indian chieftain. Words left her. Unconscious of everything but the man sitting there in blanket and feathers, she ran across the grass and threw her own blanket over him. Tears streamed down her face; her words were incoherent to the white men, but the Indians heard her cry, "My brother! My brother!"

It was indeed her brother, Cameahwait. He was deeply moved and spoke to his sister with gentle, comforting words. Then he reminded her that this was a council of men, and not the place for such a show of emotion. Still weeping, the girl returned to her place by Charbonneau and began the task of interpreting what the white men had to say.

When the council was over, Cameahwait called his sister to him, and they exchanged news of all that had happened to each during the years they had been separated. Bird Woman learned that all of her family were dead except the Chieftain,

43

another brother who was absent and the young son of her dead elder sister. Sacajawea called for the boy to be brought to her and she adopted him on the spot, naming him Bazil.

Through Sacajawea's efforts as interpreter, the two captains were able to make friendly arrangements with these Indians. Gifts were exchanged; horses and food supplies were purchased; arrangements were made for proceeding on to the western coast. During these days, when the expedition was parleying with the Indians, Sacajawea again performed a service for the white men. She had learned that the guide that had been promised them was actually planning to go off on a hunt of his own. When she made Clark understand this, the departure was forbidden, and the delay avoided.

At last everything was in readiness, and the expedition moved on. Now, again and again, Sacajawea proved her value. Each time they encountered an unfamiliar tribe, the presence of the young woman told the strange Indians that this was a peaceful expedition. No war party would hamper itself with a woman and a baby. At one stop on the Columbia River, the natives were actively hostile until the canoe carrying Sacajawea appeared. Then their whole attitude changed, and the members of the expedition were welcomed.

They arrived at the Pacific coast in mid-November. There they erected Fort Clatsop, where they remained until spring. During the winter, Bird Woman did her share of the camp work: she dried peltries, sewed up shirts and leggings, cooked and kept the cabin clean. On Christmas she gave the red-haired Captain two dozen white weasel tails which she had carefully saved for this purpose. They would add real elegance to his new elkskin hunting shirt.

The dull winter passed in days of rain and inaction. On February 11, little Pomp, as Sacajawea's boy had been nicknamed, passed his first birthday, already a seasoned traveler. On March 23, they broke camp and set out on the homeward journey.

The return trip was made swiftly and without the suspense and excitement of the outward journey. They were back at the Mandan villages in mid-August. There the captains took leave of Charbonneau, Sacajawea and little Pomp. Captain Clark wanted to take the little boy back to St. Louis with him, but the child was too young to leave his mother. The Captain made Charbonneau promise to bring his wife and child down to the city next year.

At one time it was rumored that Sacajawea had died there in the Mandan village, but few bothered to consider her fate at all. Then, in 1904, St. Louis planned a World's Fair to celebrate the hundreth anniversary of the historic trek to the Northwest. People began to think about the Indian girl who had traveled so many miles into unknown country with her baby on her back. Records, letters and reports were studied, and it was learned that, far from dying unknown and forgotten, Sacajawea had led a full and busy life.

Charbonneau had acted on Captain Clark's demand and had taken his wife and son to St. Louis. With them came Bazil, the nephew Sacajawea had adopted. Captain Clark put the boys in school. But Charbonneau did not like city life.

He mistreated Sacajawea and left to return to the mountains and rivers of the West. He died about 1839.

After several years in the city, Sacajawea left. She probably was trying to get back to her people again, but she arrived in the land of the Comanches and there married a Comanche with whom she lived twenty-five years. She bore him five children, three of whom died in infancy. When her husband died, she again set out for the mountains, taking her young son and daughter. She arrived there only to learn that her nephew and her son were at Fort Bridger in Wyoming.

Baptiste had been well educated, having been taken to Europe by a friendly prince. But like his father, he preferred the free life of the West and had come back to it.

Again Sacajawea set out for that post on the Green River. There she was welcomed by her two "sons." She remained there until the fall of 1871, a respected old woman whose experience with the Lewis and Clark expedition gave her an authority few Indian women of the West ever knew. Some authorities claim she took part in the great council of 1868 at Fort Bridger, where she is said to have urged the acceptance of the treaty offered by the United States to the hostile tribes of the region.

From 1871 until her death, Sacajawea lived with Bazil on the Shoshone Reservation on the Wind River in Wyoming. There, on April 9, 1884 she quietly died in her tipi. She was buried nearby and her grave is marked by a simple concrete shaft which bears a short inscription, giving the chief facts of her life.

No other Indian woman, save, perhaps, Pocahontas, has so captured the imagination of the American people. Her story has been told again and again, and monuments have been erected in her honor. One of these, a bronze figure of the Bird Woman with her baby on her back, stands on the State-house lawn at Bismarck, North Dakota.

CHAPTER THREE

BEAVER HATS FOR THE GENTRY
Jim Bridger (1804–1881)
and the Mountain Men

The lanky thirteen-year-old boy stood staring at the mound of earth that was slowly being piled above the coffined body of his father. Beside him, his little sister sobbed, the tears running unchecked down her freckled cheeks.

His aunt spoke briskly from behind him. "Come, Jim! Come, Sissy! No sense standing there bawling. There's work to do."

Taking his sister's hand, Jim Bridger turned away from

his father's grave. His aunt was right. There was work to do and only he to do it. How, he wondered dully, had all this happened? Within just the past year, the once happy family had been wrecked. His mother, his older brother and now his father—all had died, leaving Sissy and him to the care of their aunt. No, he corrected himself, leaving his aunt and Sissy to his care. For he was the man of the family now. It was up to him to support them.

Jim's thin shoulders straightened under the gray calico shirt. He could work; he had worked all his life. He had helped his brother do the chores around the small farm his father had purchased five years ago at Six Mile Prairie, above the bustling settlement of St. Louis. When his father had opened a tavern to supplement the farm income, Jim had helped there, serving customers, cleaning rooms and running errands.

"We'll have to sell the tavern," his aunt said suddenly. She, too, had been considering their plight. "And the farm won't keep us. It's a mighty poor bit of land. We've got skimpy times ahead, boy!"

"There's the skiff," Jim offered. "I've been thinkin' mebbe I could do better'n farming with the skiff. Ferry folks down to the wharf at St. Louie, like Pa used to for free. Only I'd charge. Might make a little."

"You might, I reckon. Folks'd rather sit in a skiff and ride down river, than slog through the swamps. And you're plenty strong and know the river."

With no more discussion than that, Jim took on the job of

ferrying travelers from the bluff at Six Mile Prairie down to the wooden wharf at the city. For a year the boy worked desperately, but he found the labor paid poorly. No one would pay more than a few cents for the short trip; some made him wait even for his small fee; some leaped from the skiff and hurried away without paying anything at all. Often he had to wait for hours at the wharf, hunting for passengers to take the return trip.

Plying his skiff along the edge of the great river, Jim came to know the picturesque men who made the Mississippi their home. Many were French-Canadians, voyageurs they called themselves, who sent their barges, pirogues, keel boats and flatboats up and down the river. Roistering, singing, swearing, fighting, dancing—they fascinated the boy. He listened to their bragging, watched their fights and yearned to be as free of responsibility and as happy in adventure, as were these, his heroes.

A year of near-starvation convinced Jim's aunt that a change must be made. She told the boy what she planned.

"Boy, we can't go on like this. We've got to give up this farm. It's no good anyhow. I kin git me a job in St. Louie—I kin take Sissy along, too. So we'll be fed and warmed, anyway. And you, Jim—well, I been down and talked to Phil Creamer. He'll take you on as 'prentice; larn you the blacksmith trade. It'll be a four year stint an' by then you'll be a man and have a trade." She sighed, her bleak eyes watching her nephew.

Over his supper bowl of mush, Jim nodded silently. He

50

was generally silent. He had found that by keeping still and listening he could learn a good deal. Years later, however, among his trapper friends, he was to earn the title of "Old Gabe" because of his constant gabbing and his tall tales told to amuse the lonely men around a campfire.

"It ires me to break up the family," his aunt said more gently. "But, boy, I can't see no other way."

Jim offered no comment. He knew Phil Creamer, a blacksmith who had many a rich man as customer; a kind man, too. It would not be a hard life, but he had failed as a provider. His Ma and Pa would have been disappointed in him. Being down in town, though, he could sort of keep an eye on his aunt and Sissy.

A few days later, Jim was established in the noisy, hot shop on Rue des Granges—the street of the barns. Now the boy was introduced to new types of people. There were the grooms from the mansions of the rich—colored men who lolled about, waiting for a horse to be shod or a buggy tire repaired. As they waited they gossiped about the food and the furnishings, the parties and the scandals that made life interesting for the onlooker. Such talk was all new to Jim but, instead of arousing envy in him, it made him impatient and angry. He could not imagine himself ever wanting to live such a life, burdened down by possessions, restricted by etiquette.

Far more to his liking were the trappers, bearded, long-haired, free-striding men, whose stained buckskins reeked with the scent of bear oil and wood smoke. By this time, 1818, St. Louis was already becoming the fur market of the

51

country. Many a fortune hunter rode out from its busy streets, north and west to trap for themselves or to trade for furs with the Indians. Before they could leave, their horses must be shod, traps repaired and other blacksmithing jobs done. Later, when they returned with a pack mule loaded with peltries, they must again visit the blacksmith.

What tales they could tell! Tales of Indians and wild animals; of prairies stretching as far as the eye could see; of mountains shining in the distance. Often Jim would forget what he was doing as his ears drank in the wonders of the far places, there to be seen by anyone with gumption enough to get up and go. Some day, Jim promised himself, I'll be one of them—as tough and mean, as loud-mouthed and dirty as the best of them! I'll see what lies out yonder.

And so the months and years slipped by, and Jim's term as apprentice was drawing to a close when, in February of 1822, a new excitement gripped the town.

The American Fur Company, headed by that rich New Yorker, John Jacob Astor, was invading St. Louis. He was going to try to take over the trade of such old timers as Manuel Lisa, Ligueste Laclede and others who for years had been bringing prosperity to the region. The St. Louis traders did not mean to sit idly by and let this happen. Already the Spaniard, Lisa, had challenged the Astorians, as the employes of the invader called themselves.

The town was agog with speculation. Partisanship was intense. Brawling and fist fights were everyday occurrences. From his vantage point of the blacksmith shop where, sooner or later, most men gathered, young Jim Bridger listened and took sides with the old traders, whom he knew.

The greatest challenge to the newcomers was one sponsored by a prominent St. Louis man General William Henry Ashley, a business man and politician. He and Major Andrew Henry joined forces and formed a new company, the Rocky Mountain Fur Company. They had money, imagination and initiative. Major Henry had already made a trip into the Upper Missouri country and knew what riches in furs could be found there.

One February day in 1822, Jim had just finished shoeing General Ashley's spirited stallion when the general's clerk, Jim Clyman, came into the blacksmith shop. Glancing up over the hoof he held between his knees, filing away a rough spot, the apprentice saw that the clerk was as dour as ever.

"He's just ready, sir!" Jim called, working vigorously.

Clyman nodded curtly and strode over to Jim's master. He held out a folded newspaper.

"Have you seen the General's advertisement?" Clyman asked.

Phil Creamer nodded. "Yep. I saw it. Got any men yet?"

Clyman shook his head. Disgust was plain on his face.

"Riff-raff! Rapscallions! Ignoramuses! That's what I get. I scour the town, but only in the taverns and on the street corners do I find men willing to give up the soft life of the city and take on adventure. It used to be different."

Jim had come to report that the horse was ready. He heard Clyman's last words.

"I'd do it, sir! Bet yore life, I'd do anything fer a taste of excitement."

Clyman's shrewd, pale eyes regarded the speaker. He saw a gangling youth, not quite eighteen years old. Already more than six feet tall, he seemed to be tough and sinewy, with heavily muscled arms and strong hands. Sharp blue-gray eyes peered out from brows too bushy for a youth of that age. The chin was firm and determined.

"Did you read the advertisement, lad?" Clyman asked.

Jim shook his head. "I cain't read, sir. I ain't had no schoolin'."

Clyman's sharp blue eyes almost disappeared as he drew his brows together in a frown. "That's the kind I get—"

Creamer interrupted. "Mebbe Jim can't read, but it's not his fault. His Ma and Pa died when Jim was jest a younker. Jim's had to work—work hard. He's a good boy."

A faint suspicion of a smile quirked Clyman's lips. "Yet he wants to go gallivanting after excitement."

Jim looked steadily at the stern-faced clerk. "I got a sister, sir! I've kept her in school, but she's growing up. She needs things. My 'prenticeship's soon up an' I got to be lookin' fer a job."

Clyman relented a little. "Well, let me read you this advertisement." He began, scarcely looking at the paper:

TO ENTERPRISING YOUNG MEN
The subscriber wishes to engage one hundred young men to ascend the Missouri River to its

source, there to be employed for one, two or three years. For particulars inquire of Major Andrew Henry, near the lead mines in the county of Washington, who will ascend with and command the party; or of the subscriber near St. Louis.

Signed, William H. Ashley

As he finished, he looked shrewdly at the youth. "Well, how does that strike you, lad?"

Jim's eyes were lively. "It'd sure pleasure me to jine!"

"Can you shoot?"

"Sure can! I'm reckoned a mighty good shot, sir!"

Clyman permitted a sour smile. "Well, that's something." He turned to the blacksmith. "If the General wants him, would you let him go now?"

Creamer hesitated, and Clyman went on with the urgency of a recruiter who has had poor luck. "Look here! I'm having trouble signing up a hundred men. If you release the lad, I'm sure General Ashley will pay you off for what's left of his time. He says it's about up."

Creamer looked at Jim and saw the eagerness in the tanned face. "Well, if the General wants him and will make good the time I lose, I won't object."

Jim thrust out his hand to grasp that of his master. "Thank 'ee, sir!" He turned to Clyman, "When kin I know?"

"Tomorrow. Maybe today. I'm taking Prince, here, up to the General's now and I'll ask about you."

55

General Ashley paid Creamer. He was eager to get his expedition upriver as early as possible in the spring to put into effect the daring scheme he and Major Henry had planned.

Until then, the trappers had followed only the streams that could be reached from the navigable rivers. They had trapped most of the game on such accessible waters. Major Henry had spent two years in the mountains near the headwaters of the Missouri, and he knew there were countless, beaver-rich streams that had never been touched. If they could send men on horseback into this virgin land, they could reap untold wealth. So the partners planned to send boats as far as possible. Then they would buy horses from the Indians and proceed into territory as yet untouched by fur hunters.

Jim found that there was more to joining this expedition than merely saying he wanted to go. General Ashley was a methodical and businesslike man. He called his men together to give them instructions on his plans. He issued lists of what each man must bring along. Jim's scanty savings went into blankets, wool shirts, leggings, his own knife and all the other personal belongings he would carry in his bundle. Traps and other equipment would be furnished by the company.

As he met the men who would be his companions, Jim was surprised at the caliber of the enlistees. He decided that Clyman's appraisal had been merely an expression of the man's usual grumpiness. One of General Ashley's favorites was a young man of education, experience and good looks Jedediah Smith, who was only a few years older than Jim. There were serious and seasoned trappers—Etienne Provot, Louis Vasquez, Black Harris; and young, intelligent newcomers to the trade, such as William Sublette and David Jackson. Jim felt shy and ignorant among these men; he admired and envied both the experience of the old hands and the education and leadership of the newcomers.

He was lonely, too. The men seemed to pair off into companionable duos, each man with a buddy. But Jim knew no one and was too shy to approach anyone. Suddenly this was changed when Louis Vasquez, whom Jim had admired secretly, approached Jim one day.

"Hi, *garcon*! Why you stand back? Come, step lively now! We must demand our portion of that tobac which the clerk now passes out. *N'est-ce pas?*" The short, dark man with a leather-brown face and piercing black eyes grasped Jim's arm and propelled him toward Clyman, who was issuing tobacco to the men.

"*Moi!*" Jim's companion went on, "*Moi*—Louis Vasquez, called Frenchy."

"Yes," Jim said grinning, "I know. I'm Jim Bridger. I—I'm new here," he added shyly.

Vasquez laughed merrily. Jim felt his loneliness melt away. Here was a friend! And from that day the two were loyal companions through all their years in the Far West.

On the sunny morning of April 3, 1822, Jim was at the dock early, his plunder bag on his shoulder, his musket in his hand, ready to set out with Major Henry on this daring and historic expedition. Louis Vasquez joined him and they went together up the gangplank of the *Enterprise*.

It was a beautiful keelboat, the pride of General Ashley. It was nearly a hundred feet long, with the cargo box reaching almost the entire length. This covered section had been fitted up so it could be used as quarters by the leaders of the expedition and could safely carry supplies on the up-trip and furs on the return.

Jim Clyman stood at the head of the gangplank to check off names. Nearby stood Major Henry, waiting to greet the men. Jim made a shrewd appraisal of the man who was to be his boss. He saw a tall, dark man with brooding eyes. The sensitive face was strengthened by a jutting chin.

The two engagés, hired trappers, found places side by side on the deck and deposited their bags. Jim straightened and looked about him. His years on the river had made him familiar with keelboats, and he appreciated the beauty and efficiency of this expensive craft. His eyes rested on the heavy iron ring embedded in the stout prow. To this the cordelle ropes could be fastened when the men had to drag the heavy vessel against the current. Jim shrugged. He knew there would be plenty of that sort of work going up the cantankerous Missouri.

Though Jim was the youngest member of the expedition, he expected and received no special treatment. He took his place at the oars, the poles and the cordelling. With gun on shoulder, he walked the river bank, hunting game for the evening meal. When the boat was drawn to shore and made fast for the night, for the river was too treacherous to navigate after dark, Jim sat with the others around the campfires and listened to the adventures the older men related with gusto and exaggeration.

The upriver trip was made without misfortune for the first two weeks, with the *Enterprise* following closely behind a smaller boat, which was laden with supplies. Then, just below old Fort Osage, some fifty miles below the mouth of the Kansas River, the lead boat struck a snag and sank. As Jim and his friends watched, horrified and helpless, ten thousand dollars worth of merchandise disappeared under the yellow waters. The crew escaped.

Jim was astounded at the calm manner in which the disaster was accepted. Without a backward glance, the crew of the lost boat joined the men on the *Enterprise* and the party went on.

They reached the mouth of the Yellowstone by the end of May. There, on a high tongue of land between the two rivers, Major Henry built his fort, mounted his cannon and waited for General Ashley, who had planned to follow the Major with more boats, men and supplies.

While the advance party waited, Jim put his time to good use. With the friendly Louis as instructor, he learned how to bait and set a beaver trap, how to skin the animal and prepare its pelt for storage. He began to pick up the jargon of the trappers and to learn the languages of the neighboring Indians. He found he was quick at this sort of thing, and soon became expert in the sign language.

It was a month before General Ashley arrived, driving a band of horses he had purchased from Indians on the way. Two days later his boat came in. There was a great feast to celebrate this event. Ashley then gave further instructions, promised to return in the spring and bade them farewell. He was going back to St. Louis.

Major Henry decided to stay at the fort till spring, putting in the time buying horses, trading with the Indians and making ready for proceeding to the heart of the fur country when spring arrived. It was a free and happy time for Jim. He found that he was suited to this sort of life, and he enjoyed every minute of it.

Before the expedition got away in the spring, Young Jedediah Smith came galloping into the fort with news that General Ashley had been attacked and defeated by the Arikara Indians. Several men had been killed, and the rest were marooned on a tiny island in the river, waiting for reenforcements. Major Henry lost no time. He selected the best eighty of his hundred men and sent them down the river to rescue the General. Jim Bridger, nineteen, was one of the chosen.

Jim felt that, for the first time in his life, he was really living. With Major Henry and the trappers, he slipped silently, under cover of night, past the Arikara villages to the island. There they were gratefully welcomed by the beleaguered men. Soon troops under Colonel Leavenworth came in from Fort Atkinson; Joseph Pilcher, president of the Missouri Fur Company sent a contingent of his own trappers; a band of warlike Sioux joined the motley assemblage.

In the three-day battle that followed, Jim had his first taste of warfare. It was a strange introduction. In spite of the plans and orders of the military men, the Sioux and Arikaras took over the fight, ignoring trappers and soldiers. When Colonel

60

Leavenworth ordered an advance, his men ran into a welter of fighting, yelling Red men. But after three days, the Arikaras signaled for a peace parley. They asked for one night in which to bury their dead. Then they would surrender everything to the soldiers.

This was Jim's first lesson in Indian strategy. During that night, the Arikaras quietly packed up women, children, wounded, dogs and supplies and stealthily disappeared. The victorious soldiers and trappers did not have a prisoner to prove their victory.

Jim couldn't help smiling. He'd have done the same thing if he'd been in their moccasins! The chagrined soldiers returned to Fort Atkinson. General Ashley returned to St. Louis to collect more money and supplies. Jedediah Smith and a small band set out due west. Jim was named to go with Major Henry's party on foot back up the river to their fort.

In the shuffling of men, Jim had been assigned a new companion, Old Hugh Glass. This tough and crusty old trapper had small respect for anyone as young as Jim, though he did have to admit that the youth's gun was as good as or better than his own. But the admission was not pleasant, and the two had little in common, though Jim rather liked the old fellow.

Five days away from the Arikara village, Jim was out hunting with Old Hugh and another companion. They were supposed to stay together—both Indians and wild animals were less dangerous when met by even two or three armed men. But Old Hugh was not one to obey orders. He struck off alone through a thicket, looking for game. As he threshed along, he almost stumbled on a huge female grizzly bear.

Hugh knew only too well what that bear meant. Of all the dangers they had to face, the trappers feared a grizzly most. A female grizzly was worst of all. Scared as he was, Hugh took aim and fired, but his shot only wounded the huge beast. Screaming with rage and pain, she threw herself upon the old man before he had a chance to reload. Her terrible claws ripped his body; her great fangs tore at his head and shoulder.

Hugh's screams of pain and terror brought the others run-

62

ning. For a moment they stood helpless, unable to shoot for fear of hitting the man, not the animal. Jim had his gun up, his eyes watching for a chance. Finally he saw an opening and he pressed the trigger. The great beast fell.

Jim and his companion rushed to the victim, who lay unconscious in a pool of blood. It seemed impossible that he was alive, but the heart still beat feebly under the torn flesh.

Jim looked at his companion. "We cain't move him, nohow. What kin we do?" In spite of himself his voice shook. Only a week before, he had seen and smelled fresh blood for the first time. Even that had been less horrible than this.

His companion, who has never been identified in the reports of the tragedy, knew what was expected. They should stay here till the old man died, then bury him and hasten to catch up with the others and report the accident. But he did not explain this to Jim. Instead he assumed an air of finality.

"He's gone, Jim. No use us hanging 'round till this she-bear's mate or some skulking Redskin finds us and wipes us out too. Let's git back to the Major an' tell him how Old Hugh snuck off by hisself and got killed."

What went through the heart and mind of Jim Bridger can only be imagined. Whatever it was, he acted on his companion's suggestion and reported to Major Henry that when they had left, Old Hugh was dead. According to the custom of the mountains, the expedition moved on.

Old Hugh Glass was not dead. He regained consciousness to find himself abandoned, almost naked, and without gun, knife or ammunition. Jim's companion had taken the old man's

63

belongings to support the story of his death. He lay there for awhile, gathering strength. Then he set out, crawling on his hands and knees, for the nearest post, Fort Kiowa, a hundred miles away.

How he made the terrible journey has inspired many a song and story. At the Fort he was nursed back to health. Then he set out to find the men who had abandoned him and to take revenge upon them.

The Christmas season came when Jim was at Fort Henry.

It was the last Christmas the young man would celebrate before leaving his teens. He was not much in the mood for a celebration. He had been haunted by misgivings all these past months.

It was difficult to be moody when trappers and Indians were coming in jolly bands to observe the holiday with extra food and drink, tobacco and music. The Fort took on a festive air as the men ate and drank, danced and sang, and told their favorite yarns. In spite of himself, Jim was caught up in the gaiety.

Suddenly the door was pushed open and a pallid ghost stumbled into the noisy, smoke-filled room. The noise stopped as the wild, rough men stared at the apparition. Old Hugh Glass, returned from the grave, had come seeking revenge!

Jim's face whitened under the tan. He drew back into a corner. The old man's eyes, roving over the crowd, came to him. Stumbling and muttering, Hugh advanced toward the cowering youth. Through the deathly stillness the old man's voice cried, "I've come to kill ye, younker!"

Involuntarily, Jim raised his hands to ward off the knife. But Hugh's hands dropped to his side. His voice broke as he went on, "No! I cain't do it. I kin see ye warn't to blame—a younker, a greenhorn. But t'other! I'll git him!"

He swayed on his feet, and Jim leaped forward and helped the old man to a seat by the fire. The revelry was forgotten as the trappers gathered around to hear the wondrous tale of the hundred-mile journey on hands and knees, without food or drink save what could be garnered from bush and puddle. Jim put off telling the old man that their companion on that terrible day had deserted the trappers and returned to Fort Atkinson to become a soldier.

That night—the Christmas he was nineteen—Jim Bridger became a man. It is indicative of the respect in which he was held that all through the years he was never taunted with the story of his one dishonorable act. He became one of the truly great mountain men, trapping beaver throughout the Far West. He is credited with discovering the Great Salt Lake.

When the fur trade faded, Jim Bridger built a fort on the Green River, in what is now southern Wyoming. Here, he supplied emigrant trains moving West, traded with the Indians of the region, assisted United States troops sent into the area at different times and married his Indian wives. He died on July 17, 1881, at the age of seventy-seven. He was first buried on private ground, but, in 1904, his body was removed to Mt. Washington cemetery in Kansas City, Missouri. A granite shaft bearing his chiseled portrait and a brief biography mark his grave.

Fort Bridger, in southern Wyoming, is now a museum of western history, small and unpretentious, but visited by hundreds every year. The famous trapper's name is preserved in Bridger's Pass, a way over the Continental Divide discovered by Jim and used by the Pony Express and the Union Pacific Railroad. Legend and history have made it one of the most familiar names in the story of the Far West.

CHAPTER FOUR

LEGENDARY SCOUT
Kit Carson (1809–1868)
and the Santa Fe Trail

The boy stood in the door of the little saddler's shop and watched the wagon train move slowly down the dusty road. It was September, and fall had already colored the trees around the frontier town of Franklin, Missouri. The smell of autumn was in the air; autumn, with its reminder of wood fires burning, sweet smoke rising and the Indian colors that would soon dress the woodland.

67

Indian colors! Indian country!, the boy was thinking. His eyes moved from the wagon train to the dusky, blanketed figures squatted along the roadside. There were other figures there—bearded mountain men in greasy, smelly buckskins, with knives in their belts and their rifles close at hand.

From inside the shop, Dave Workman, the saddler, spoke to his apprentice.

"Mooning agin, Kit? Come, git to work, boy! I reckon the smell of far places is enticing to young blood, but yore bound to me for four more years. After that, boy, you kin go where you please."

Kit turned back into the shop. Dave was right. He must stay here and work. His folks had planned to make a lawyer of him, but since his Pa had died the family had been forced to give up that idea. So he'd been bound to Dave Workman to learn the saddler's trade.

He went to the saddletree and began to punch awl holes and lace in the leather thongs to finish the skirt of the saddle he had been working on. Through the open door came the shouts and comments of the loafers.

"Give my regyards to Santa Fee!"

"Goodby, old hoss! Come back with plenty of Mexie gold!"

"Kiss one of them pretty senoritas fer me!"

As Kit punched and laced, the keen, sharp smell of new leather seemed to change magically to the smother of dust. The old yearning hardened within him.

That evening, when Workman had closed the shop and gone home, Kit did not fling himself down on the pallet at

68

the rear of the room. Instead, he jerked his blanket from the straw tick and flung upon it his few belongings: a ragged shirt, a pair of sox and cowhide shoes; some stale cheese, half a loaf of bread and a handful of hickory nuts. He folded the ends of the blanket together to make a snug bundle.

From its place on the wall above his pallet he took down his father's old muzzle-loader, his powder horn and leather bag of shot and patches. He had been using this clumsy firearm since he had been knee-high to a 'possum. At twelve, he had won the shooting matches for boys around his home in Boon's Lick. Now he took time to load the musket by the light of a candle. No telling what a man might meet along the river road in the dark of night. He carefully measured out powder, poured it down the muzzle, wet a patch and wrapped it around a ball. He rammed this down to rest upon the powder. Now let man or beast try any tricks—he was ready! With powder horn and bag secure at his belt, musket in hand and bundle on his shoulder, Kit set out.

He knew the caravan would camp at Hardman's ferry, six miles above Franklin. During the past year at Workman's he had done many a repair job for the Santa Fe trains. Just this morning he'd mended a stirrup strap for one of Captain West's men—a good-natured fellow who had filled the boy's ears with tales of the adventures to be found on the trail to Mexico.

The September moon was bright and the sky unclouded as Kit hurried along, whistling under his breath. As he drew near the campsite he became very cautious. It would never do to go barging in, startling the guards. He might get killed for such foolishness. Kit paused in the shadow of a tree to survey the camp. Yep! There were guards walking slowly up and down beside the string of wagons. Cap'n West sure knew his business! Plenty of river rats would like to lay hands on some of that cargo.

As Kit watched, there was a stealthy movement among the trees, not far from where he stood. His eyes, trained to superior keenness by his long experience in the woods, pierced the shadows and saw skulking figures moving stealthily toward the camp. Over by the wagons, the two sentries met and paused, their backs to the trees, to light their hand rolled cigarettes. The shadowy figures leaped out into the moonlight, running lightly toward the unsuspecting guards.

Kit didn't pause to think. He moved swiftly. Pouring flash powder into the priming pan of his gun, he put on the cap lock and hoisted the heavy weapon to position. Strong as he was, with arm and shoulder muscles corded from heavy work, it was a real job to hold and aim the old firearm, but Kit was accustomed to it. He took aim and pulled the trigger.

The report sounded like a cannon. The guards wheeled. The sleeping men leaped to their feet, guns ready. The thieves turned and ran, trying to escape, but the traders were after them, guns barking.

Kit felt a heavy hand on his shoulder. He was dragged forward and flung down in front of the captain.

"I caught one of the dogs," a rough voice declared. "A pup, rather. Ain't dry behind the ears."

"Who are you?" the captain asked harshly. He yanked the

gun out of Kit's hand. "Aimed to bring down one of my men with this old blunderbuss, eh?"

"No, sir. I saw those men sneakin' up on yore camp. It was them I aimed at. Christopher Carson, sir, called Kit," he added.

"A likely story! And what were you doing, anyway? Sneaking around here in the middle of the night?"

"I came to ask you fer a job, sir. I want to go West. It was so late when I got here, I thought I'd better wait till morning—"

A big, broad-shouldered fellow came up. Kit saw that it was the man whose stirrup he had repaired. He looked at Kit, grinned and said, "That's right, Booshway. He was helpin' Dave Workman. Fixed a stirrup strap fer me, he did."

"A runaway apprentice, eh?" the captain said, frowning. "That's bad."

"Aw, Cap'n," the newcomer said comfortably. Kit noticed that he had substituted the more complimentary term of Captain for the familiar "booshway" used by the men to designate the "boss" of an expedition. "You know how it is with these younkers! Standing by, watching the caravans go past. I'd say—give him a chance, Cap'n."

The captain hesitated. "It's against the law, Broaddus."

"I don't reckon the law reaches to Santa Fe, sir!" Kit put in boldly. Broaddus guffawed. "He's a quick one, he is! I'll wager he kin hold his own. And he did you a favor, Cap'n."

The captain scrutinized the boy. "You're not very big. How old are you? What can you do?"

71

"I'm strong, though," Kit said sturdily. "I'm sixteen, seventeen come Christmas Eve. I can shoot. I'm the best shot hereabouts, sir. I'll bring in more'n I eat."

The captain still studied the boy. He saw a short, stocky youngster with a shock of light hair and eyes that did not waver as they gazed steadily, but not impudently, into his own.

"I kin use a boy, Cap'n," Broaddus urged.

"Very well. You're hired. Five dollars a month. Joe Broaddus will be your boss, but if there's any funny business, you'll hear from me direct. Punishments in this train are fines for minor offenses; whippings when they're deserved." He turned and strode away. He gave a look at the thieves, now bound securely to the wagons. In the morning they'd be flogged and turned over to the sheriff at Franklin. The wagon train could not be delayed to see that they were properly punished.

"Where's yore plunder bag, boy?" Broaddus asked.

"Yonder. I dropped it when I took aim."

"Get it an' come along. I sleep over there." He nodded toward the last of the wagons.

Kit got his bundle and followed his benefactor. He unrolled his blanket and lay down. The camp grew quiet, but Kit could not sleep. He lay staring up at the night sky, thinking of his past and his future. How long had he dreamed of going West? Probably almost since he was born that Christmas Eve of 1809. It had taken him long enough to come to it. But he was on his way at last.

He was awakened by the shout, "Turn out! Turn Out!"

72

He leaped to his feet. It was gray dawn, not yet day. Near-by his friend sat up, yawning and scratching.

"Glad to see ye kin wake up all of a piece!" Broaddus said. "Come along, boy, and give me a hand with the horses."

Kit scrambled up and followed the man, eager to learn what was required of him. The first thing, he saw, was to loosen the animals from their picket stakes and drive them out to graze.

"Whilst they fill up fer the day, we kin do the same," Broaddus explained.

Kit was in the horse guard mess with Broaddus and four other men, Gouge Eye, Sam, Pete and Old Boot. As Kit expected, they greeted him with jocular comments about his size. Kit said nothing. All his life folks had spouted off because he was a bit short, until they saw him handle Betsy Lou. That old musket told them what Kit, himself, wouldn't bother to say, and they soon shut up.

It took most of the day to get the caravan across the river, so they camped there again that night. But on the second morning Kit heard the shout he had longed to hear, "Stre—e—e-tch out!" The wagons rumbled slowly into their designated positions, and the long line began to snake southwest toward Mexico.

At midday there was a brief stop for a meal, but no time for resting. In the afternoon, Kit got permission from Broaddus to borrow a horse so he could go buffalo hunting with some hunters from the train. To the surprise of everyone, the boy proved his claim as a marksman, bringing down one of

the huge, shaggy beasts. The hunters gathered around to carve away the choice parts, tossing exclamations of praise at Kit, who assumed just the right pose of modesty and nonchalance.

Resting time came after supper, when the men lolled at ease around the campfires, smoking and telling yarns. Kit listened to these tales, knowing that much was exaggeration. Still, there was something to be learned from every one. When old Gouge Eye told how an arrow had blinded him one night when he had been warming himself by a fire, Kit made a mental note never to make such a target of himself. When Alez Temple told how he had driven off a band of Comanches, brandishing his gun like a club because it was too wet to fire, Kit determined always to sleep with his own musket in his blanket with him, where it would be dry and ready.

The caravan moved on at a pleasant pace, untroubled by storms or Indians. The only nuisance was the wolves which

gathered every night around the camp, howling, driven frantic
by the smell of the raw buffalo meat in the wagons. Broaddus hated the wolves, and he would send a shot out into the
darkness to scare his tormentors away.

One night, the second week out, the wolves were particularly annoying, and Broaddus's shots seemed to have no effect.
He went to the nearest wagon, where he had stowed an extra
gun, reached in and pulled out the weapon. As he did so, the
lock caught on something, causing it to become partially set.
If he had not been so upset by the wolves, he would have been

more careful in freeing the weapon, but he gave it a jerk. The hammer came down and fired the gun. The ball went through his arm.

Kit, who had been awakened by the ruckus and had followed the man, ran for the booshway. A crowd gathered. The men took turns examining the wound and suggesting what should be done.

"Don't none of you know what to do?" cried Kit. For once his usually cool voice showed panic.

The wound was washed, whiskey was poured into it and into the victim; a clean rag was tied around the mutilated arm. All night long, Kit could hear his friend moaning with pain. By morning, Broaddus had a high fever.

Kit went among the teamsters, begging them to do something.

"Might try baccy juice," someone suggested. This was done, but the wound grew steadily worse.

Finally Captain West announced grimly, "That arm will have to come off!"

The men shuddered and drew away.

"Some one will have to do the job!" West went on. He looked about him. "You men who are his messmates should be the best. You know him and he knows you." His eyes went over the cowering group. "You, Pete! And Sam. And—Kit! It'll take three, I know. After you remove the arm, cauterize the wound with a red hot iron!" He turned away.

"Yeah!" Pete grunted. "Booshway can't stand it, neither."

Kit thought that he, too, couldn't stand it. He gulped down

the nausea that soured his throat. If this was part of the job he'd taken on, he would do it without any fuss.

Grimly the three went to work with a razor, a saw and a red hot king bolt.

When the job was done and the patient was resting, Kit went out, away from the camp and sat down by himself. Now he let the tears and the nausea take over. For an hour he gave way to his misery. Then he dried his eyes, blew his nose and went back to camp.

Kit took over much of his friend's work, and Broaddus recovered rapidly. As they rode along, side by side, the man instructed the boy in the ways of the Taos Traders, the Santa Fe caravans, and the hostile Indians that bedeviled the whites.

"Them Injuns think they have a danged good right to kill us off an' take our plunder," he explained. "They figger we're trespassing on their land and killing their buffler. But we try to teach 'em better." He patted his gun. "And even if we do lose now and then, we still make money fer the booshway and the company. Why, d'ye know, Kit, only a couple of years ago, Bill Becknell's big caravan came into St. Looey with near a hundred thousand dollars in gold and silver and ten thousand in furs. Fer just one trip, mind ye. Ah, the Santa Fe Trail! You stick to it, Kit, an' you'll be rich some day."

"But I don't aim to be a Santa Fe trader!" Kit protested. "I aim to be a scout—a mountain man!"

"Mounting men! Wagh!" Broaddus spit disdainfully.

When finally the caravan entered Santa Fe, Kit looked about him and felt keen disappointment. Where were the gold and silver, the Spanish jewels, the beautiful senoritas? Before him lay some scattered, small adobe houses, streets of red sand, unkempt children and mangy dogs. A few sombreroed Mexicans sauntered about or sat in the shade with their knees under their chins. It was not Kit's dream of a magical city.

Since Kit did not plan to return with the caravans, he bade the captain, Broaddus and his messmates goodby. With his scanty wages in his pocket, he set out to find a band of trappers which he could join. He had no luck in Santa Fe and was advised to go to Taos, some eighty miles northeast of the capital. There, he was told, Ewing Young was the man to see. If anyone was sending out trappers, it would be Young.

Ewing Young was not sending out any parties till spring. Still, he liked the looks of Kit and gave him a temporary job as cook for one of his groups that was waiting out the winter. Kit had never tried cooking for anyone but himself, but he accepted the job and did his best. A friendly old fellow, Bill Kincaid, gave the boy a place to sleep and began teaching him Spanish.

"Ye cain't thrive hereabout lees'n ye kin palaver with these Mexies!" Kincaid explained.

Kit learned rapidly and enjoyed using his new skill. But his hope of becoming a trapper diminished.

"Unless yore hired by a company," Kincaid explained, "you have to furnish yore own fixin's—not jest gun and powder, but buckskins an' wool shirt, yore traps, an' most of all yore own hoss."

"I'll get them," Kit said.

When a chance came for him to use his Spanish to get a better job, he resigned as cook and hired out as an interpreter for a caravan going all the long way to El Paso and Chihuahua.

Seeing Chihuahua, in Old Mexico, was an exciting experience for the boy. Like Santa Fe, it was the capital of a Mexican province, but it was older and far grander than the one he had just left. Here, for the first time in his life, Kit saw a great, domed cathedral, gardens, statues, paved streets and other signs of a civilization he had never dreamed of. But the work of an interpreter was dull, and, before long, Kit was willing to settle for a more humble job as teamster for a caravan returning to Taos.

Back in the New Mexican town, he still could not find employment as a trapper, and for the first time his courage and determination failed. He decided to return to his home in Missouri and obtained a job as teamster with a caravan going east. As he drove along, he began to take stock of himself. Was this the stuff he was made of? Was he so weak he would give out at the first strain?

Halfway back to Missouri, the caravan was fording the Arkansas River when it met another caravan on its way to New Mexico. Kit went to his boss and asked to be released from his job. Then he trotted over to the boss of the westering train and hired on as a mere chore boy. He got back to Taos so broke that he was actually in need of a shirt. He hired out at once as teamster for a train going to El Paso.

Kit was terribly unhappy. He felt that he was a failure at

seventeen. He had been unable to do the one thing he wanted to do, become a trapper. His fortune was at the lowest ebb but it improved. When the caravan returned to Taos, Ewing Young was about to send an expedition to the mountains. He was ready to hire Kit.

Ewing Young, himself, was to be the booshway of this expedition. He had sent out an earlier company, but it had been attacked by Apaches and many of his men slain. Now he wished to teach those Indians a lesson.

"Can you pick up an Indian trail?" he asked Kit.

"Yes sir. I kin pick up any trail," the youth answered.

He was as good as his word, and before many days he could point out to his employer where the Apaches were camped across a low valley near Salt River.

A consultation was held to decide how to attack the Indians. Captain Young decided that he would conceal most of his men among some neighboring trees. Then he would send a small party toward the Apache camp to decoy the braves into chasing them into the ambush. Kit volunteered to be one of those to ride on this dangerous assignment.

The ruse worked. When the Apaches saw a handful of horsemen approaching, they let out a war whoop, leaped upon their horses and came loping toward Young's men. The trappers turned and fled. The Indians, riding in true Apache fashion—each warrior slung alongside the body of his mount and shooting from under the animal's neck, dashed headlong after the fleeing trappers. When they were within the trap,

80

the guns spat. Taken wholly by surprise, the Apaches turned and fled, leaving dead and wounded behind.

Ewing Young was pleased with Kit's action during this escapade. The youth was cool and collected. He showed absolutely no fear, and his aim was magnificent. For awhile now, trappers passing this way would be safe.

For the next eight years, Kit was just what he had dreamed of being—a mountain man. His name became a legend. He trapped all over the western region and became acquainted with all the famous mountain men of the era.

When the heydey of the fur trade was over, Kit became known as the Guardian of the Plains. He was employed by the United States as a scout and often rescued trade caravans or emigrant trains from Indian attack. He had a natural knack for handling Indians which made him invaluable whenever they caused trouble.

In 1843, Kit met John C. Frémont, who was then looking for a guide on one of his many expeditions to the Far West. Frémont employed the noted scout, and for many years they were friends as well as employer-employe. When this work was over, Kit settled on a farm near Taos, the city he really loved best. From this place he acted as Government agent for the Indians, serving the Utes so well that they called on him whenever they were in trouble. In the summer of 1867, when Kit was fifty-seven years old and ill, the Utes begged him to go to Washington on their behalf in the dispute over their Colorado lands where gold and silver had been found by white prospectors. Kit went, but when he returned he found that his wife had died, leaving him with six children, the youngest a tiny baby.

Kit had fallen in love with a Mexican girl, Josepha Jaramillo, some twenty-five years before and had become a Catholic in order to marry her. Now, fearing his death was near, he considered what was best to do for his motherless children. He appointed Tom Boggs, a friend and neighbor, as their guardian, knowing he would take good care of them.

He died at Fort Lyon on May 23, 1868 and was buried in the little cemetery at Taos, New Mexico.

The name Kit Carson has become almost synonymous with all that was admirable in the trappers and scouts of the Early West. His name has been preserved in other ways: in Carson City, the capital of Nevada; Carson Lake, Carson River and Carson Sink, all in the same state. There is Carson County in Texas and Carson village in North Dakota; Carson Pass in California and Carson Peak in Colorado.

Wherever there are statues of western historical characters, there is almost certain to be one of Kit Carson. His likeness stands out on the "This is the Place" monument east of Salt Lake City. New Mexico has the Carson National Forest. On one of the islands in the Great Salt Lake there is a cross carved on a rock—a memento left behind by Kit when he explored the island with Frémont in the fall of 1843.

CHAPTER FIVE

SCHOOLMARM IN ZION
Mary Jane Dilworth (1831–1877)
and the Mormon Trek

The old river boat nosed its way up the Mississippi. All along the rail the passengers crowded, peering ahead. They knew they were drawing close to their goal and were eager to catch sight of it. Then the boat rounded a point of land and there it was!

Fourteen-year-old Mary Jane Dilworth felt her heart

84

pound with excitement. She leaned forward across the rail, staring, wide-eyed. From the west, across the river and the wooded plains of Iowa, the late afternoon sun sent its slanting rays to bathe the city that rose in terraced steps from the river bank. Mary Jane gave an exclamation of delight and pointed. Crowning a hill to the east was the Temple, gleaming and gilded by the sun.

"Oh! How beautiful!"

Beside her, her mother, Eliza Dilworth, smiled. "Nauvoo, the Beautiful. How well it is named!"

Now the boat had edged to the small wooden dock and a gangway was being lowered. The passengers crowded forward, all eager to set foot on land again after their long and wearisome journey. Mary Jane, her mother and brother, John, and her sisters, Martha Ann, Elizabeth and Maria hurried along with the others. But they couldn't help staring over the rail, down at the dock where a welcoming group waited.

"I see them!" Mary Jane exclaimed. "There's Rebecca and Levi—yes, Mother! There's Lavina, too—and Ann! Oh, I can't wait!"

They pushed ahead, scurried down the gangway and into the arms of the waiting women.

"Mother! Oh, how glad we are to see you at last!" Rebecca cried. Mary Jane was astonished to see tears in her sister's eyes. Rebecca had never been one to cry for happiness. Her tall husband shook Eliza's hand.

"We thought you'd never get here," he murmured.

There were kisses and exclamations of greeting. Eliza

hugged her grandsons, Samuel, William, Evans and Caleb. "How you boys have grown!" she said, holding them close.

Trunks, chests, carpet bags and bundles had been dumped down onto the dock. Other passengers were picking up their luggage, and Eliza pointed out the things that belonged to her and her children.

"All that!" William Bringhurst exclaimed. There was a slight frown on his face as he glanced at his wife, Ann.

"Don't worry, Uncle Will!" twelve-year-old Evans said. "We boys can manage it easy!" His brother Caleb and his two cousins ran to pick up their share.

"It isn't that," Will Bringhurst said quietly. "It's just that we're going to be loaded—"

"Not now, Will!" Ann begged. "Later! There's plenty of time."

They started up the street from the wharf, a chattering group—a family reunited after years of separation. Mary Jane and Maria found themselves together behind the others.

"How neat it is—the city!" Mary Jane said. "All the streets so straight—the whole town laid out in absolutely square blocks!"

"But so quiet!" Maria whispered. "Look, Mary Jane! Half the houses look empty—some are even half burned, it looks like!"

Their nephew Evans heard them. "That's the mobbers," he told them and his voice was bitter. "They've been burning and stealing—"

86

Levi Riter was talking to the girls' mother. "We've been packed and ready to go for weeks. Just waiting for you—"

"But when you wrote you said the Saints weren't leaving till fall—"

"That's what we planned. But the mobbers got busy and President Young, our leader, decided we should go as soon as possible. He led the first company away last February—and folks have been leaving ever since."

There was a great deal to be discussed that evening at Levi Riter's cabin—questions to be asked and answered; news items to be exchanged. A Pennsylvania Quaker family, Eliza Dilworth and her children had listened to missionaries who came bringing word of a new religion, a restored Gospel. It had attracted the Dilworths, as it had many of their neighbors in that quiet countryside, and they had all decided to join the new church. Those who were old enough had been baptized by the "elders." The older girls, Rebecca, Lavina and Ann, had married neighboring young men, also converts. They had gone to New York, where the church had been organized. But troubles came and the new Saints, as the Mormans called themselves, had to leave their homes. Mary Ann's sisters followed—from New York to Ohio; from Ohio to Missouri; from Missouri to Illinois.

Even there, where they had expected to find sanctuary, the Saints had run into difficulties with their neighbors, who feared their growing political and religious power. Almost two years before this April evening, Joseph Smith, the founder of the new church, and his brother Hyrum had been assassinated. One of the most influential men, Brigham Young, had assumed the leadership of the frightened people. He knew they must move, and he was determined to go where the murdered founder had dreamed of going—to the desert lands of the Far West. But first, they would build their Temple, as Joseph Smith had planned.

For nearly two years they had worked, erecting the shining Temple on the crest of the hill where its gleaming walls could be see from afar. They also had been busy planting crops and harvesting them, drying food and collecting supplies, getting ready for the journey into the unknown West. All the while, hundreds of converts from the East and from foreign lands were pouring into the little city so they would be on hand to go with the Saints to the new Zion.

Petitioned by her daughters and urged by her own wish to share in the blessings she felt sure were in store, Eliza had found it difficult to wait till Maria, her youngest, was old enough to take on such a long and difficult trip. When Maria was twelve, Eliza packed up her belongings, and, with her five younger daughters and her one son, she came at last to the City Beautiful. She was ready and willing to go on, though she had not anticipated such a speedy departure.

For the next few days, all was hurry and bustle at the Riter home. Although, as Levi had said, they had been packed and ready for some time, the coming of seven more people with their baggage and the necessity of finding wagons and supplies for them created a great deal of extra work. Still, Mary Jane and Maria found time to wander about the deserted city, staring into empty windows, wondering at abandoned gardens, and gazing in awe at the Temple.

Mary Jane was aquiver with mixed emotions. She was saddened by the devastation in the city. She was worried about the scant supply of food she and her family had brought with them. She was filled with religious exaltation when her brother-in-law William Bringhurst took her and Maria to the edge of the mighty Mississippi and baptized them into the church.

She tingled with excitement at the thought of setting out toward the West. She would stand on the hill, below the Temple, and gaze across the river, across the miles and miles of wooded plain stretching into the blue distance. Her heart would pound. Soon she would be traveling through that tall grass, under those ancient trees, on her way across Iowa.

Finally all was ready and the family set out: Eliza, now fifty-five years old; Rebecca and Levi Riter with their two boys, Samuel, eleven, and William, nine; Lavina, whose husband, Charles Harper, had gone on ahead; Ann and William Bringhurst with Evans and Caleb—named for his grandfather; Harriet, Martha, Elizabeth, Mary Jane, Maria and the lone brother of all these sisters, twenty-one-year-old John.

It was beautiful weather now and the prairie was bright with wild flowers; the smell of wild grass was sweet to the travelers' nostrils.

Mary Jane, Maria and the four little boys couldn't bear the inactivity of the wagons. They ran barefooted through the damp grass alongside the vehicles. They frolicked, gathered wild flowers and thought they were having a picnic all day long, for the first few days. Then it began to rain, and they huddled under the canvas wagon tops and tried to amuse themselves.

"I'll tell you what!" Mary Jane exclaimed one afternoon when the boys were becoming noisy with boredom. "Let's play school. I'll be the teacher——"

"Oh, yeah!" Evans cried. "I'll bet you can't teach me anything! I've been to school in Nauvoo. I can read——"

Mary Jane dug down into her own private belongings and brought out a book——a small, blue-backed speller.

"All right!" she agreed. "Let's hear you spell Mississippi!"

"That's easy. M-I-double S, I-double S, I-double PP-I!" he chanted.

"Wrong, smarty! 'double P-P-I!' You'd have three p's! and whoever heard of such a thing!"

"I'll play if you'll tell us a story," said eight-year-old William.

"I'll tell you a story after you have lessons," Mary Jane agreed.

She sat the five youngsters in front of her and began with her most winning expression, "Let's start with a song. You choose, Evans!"

To the surprise of everyone, the afternoon flew past. Maria, who was not as fond of books as her sister, discovered it could be fun to read the stories in Mary Jane's books——if Mary Jane would help with the hard words. Evans and Samuel both found that they really liked arithmetic; Caleb and

90

William were willing to work in order to hear the story with which their teacher rewarded them.

From that day on, some of the time each afternoon was spent on lessons. It was not a rigid schedule. Generally, they only studied through the hottest hours after their midday stop. Interruptions were sometimes permitted, especially at the camps where they spent several days resting, washing clothes and baking bread.

Mary Jane was surprised to find that, every now and then, they would come to a sort of settlement, a place where those ahead had stopped, built cabins and planted gardens so that latecomers could have fresh food. Such places had been given names—Garden Grove, Mount Pisgah, Cutler's Park.

At this last stop, the Dilworth's discovered that Lavina's husband had volunteered to go with the Mormon Battalion to help Colonel Stephen W. Kearny take California for the American settlers in that region. They had left early in June.

Lavina wept. She had hoped to see her husband again either there or at their next stop. Now she did not know when they would meet again.

The Saints reassured her. "President Young promised that not a man would be killed in battle," they told her. "The President of the United States sent a Captain Allen here to get a battalion of five hundred men. At first we didn't want to let them go, but President Young said we ought to. He found a flag someplace, hoisted it to the top of a stripped tree trunk, and the men responded. Don't worry. Your husband will be safe, and blessed for going."

On the family moved, past Cutler's Park and on to Council Bluffs on the Missouri River. Mary Jane stared when they came in sight of this place. She knew that the Saints had decided to winter there. When they had arrived, it had been too late in the year for them to attempt the desert and mountains ahead. So she had expected a sort of settlement, perhaps like Mount Pisgah. This was different!

Across the river from where their wagons had stopped were some lovely, rounded hills. Each of these seemed to be a picnic ground—white canvas tents and wagon tops glittered in the sunshine; the bright colors of calico shirts, dresses and sunbonnets sparkled gaily. From the east side, where the flat ground beside the river was crowded with wagons and carts waiting to be ferried across, the opposite hills gave promise of a pleasant, bustling village.

Mary Jane was not disappointed when, finally, their wagons had been ferried across the river and they had been pulled up the slope into the encampment.

It was a regular "town." The softly rounded hills, she discovered, circled a fine spring of sparkling water. On each of the hills a square had been marked out, and, as each wagon came up, the driver was shown his place along the sides of this square. The wagons were drawn up in double rows, to leave a roomy street or passageway between them. Here and there among the wagons were tents, but they, too, preserved the outline of the square.

The inside of the quadrangle was left empty to provide ventilation for the inner row of wagons. The streets between

92

were covered by a leafy lattice work and were very clean. Mary Jane was soon to discover that these shady walks were where the children played during the day. Sick people were placed there to enjoy the cool, fresh air. In the evenings, everyone strolled along, meeting friends, gossiping and enjoying the neighborliness they were too busy to savor during the day.

At Council Bluffs, the older boys had plenty of work to do and their lessons came to an end. At night, the cattle were herded into a high-walled enclosure, but during the day the boys took them out to graze away from the camp. The boys also cut wild hay and brought it into camp, chopped wood, ran errands and picked wild berries. The girls, too, were kept busy, washing and ironing clothing for their group. They made jam and jelly, using great iron kettles over open camp fires. They milked the cows and churned the butter. They took care of the children and of the old and the sick.

Because Mary Jane had a knack with young children, she soon found herself the nursemaid for the dozen smaller children on the "street" where her family's wagons had been placed. Because she found it easy to amuse them by teaching them, her job became more that of a teacher than of a nurse. She had a few books, but they were too advanced for her small charges. So she began by amusing them with rhymes and pictures to teach them their ABC's. She often made up the rhymes. She drew pictures with charcoal on the tail gates of wagons, on a newly shaved bit of wood or on a piece of clean bark.

She told stories, sang songs and played games till she had

used up all the amusements she knew. At her wits end, one day the idea of teaching the children to read came to her. With a piece of charcoal she drew a capital A; she added a couple of lines at the apex to represent the stakes of a wigwam. Under the crossbar she sketched a child's head peeking out.

"See, children! A is a tent—a big, pointed tent! There is a little girl. I wonder where she went!" And she rubbed out the picture of the child.

It took only a little encouragement to get the children—some of them scarcely more than babies—to chant with her, "A is a tent! A great big tent!" She let them hold the charcoal and try to draw the "tent." She went along the street marking capital A's on endgates. The children tagged along, singing.

Now it was a natural step to, "B is a stick with bundles on its back!" And, "C is a snake with its mouth open wide." Mary Jane was having fun, and so were the children. As they drew letters and chanted their sing-song, passing people stopped to watch.

One day President Young, himself, paused to listen. His shrewd eyes took in all that Mary Jane was doing; his ruddy face beamed.

"I have a boy that could use some of that learning," he said with a chuckle.

Mary Jane flushed, but she answered, "Send him over, sir! There is always room for one more."

So six-year-old Perry Decker, the son of one of Brigham Young's wives, came to Mary Jane's classes.

The autumn passed and winter came—a dreadful winter

for the Saints in their hastily built shelters on the bank of the Missouri River. Hundreds were sick; scores died. The problem of caring for restless children, confined to crowded quarters by the terrible cold, became a major difficulty.

One day Mary Jane's sister Harriet suggested, "Why don't you go on with the lessons you started with the boys last summer on the way out here? The children are getting to be a nuisance cooped up all day long. And they really should be learning something. I don't want them to grow up absolutely uneducated!"

Mary Jane agreed. One of the mottoes of her church was "The Glory of God is intelligence." The leaders had established schools for the elders in Nauvoo; parents had been constantly encouraged to send their children to the classes taught by educated men and women in the various settlements where they had made their homes. But here in winter quarters, with so much work to be done and so much sickness, there had been scant time and little available help. Most of the children were being taught at home, somehow.

Mary Jane's brothers-in-law had managed to build substantial cabins against the winter's cold. Her sister Rebecca turned the one large room of her cabin over to Mary Jane for the morning hours. There her four nephews and a few children from nearby huts and tents came each day. Fifteen-year-old Mary Jane was their teacher.

Everyone in winter quarters had his heart set on reaching the new Zion, lying somewhere in the distant West. While Mary Jane kept a small group of children at their lessons, others were preparing for the long journey to be undertaken in the spring. In April of 1847, Brigham Young set out with the advance company of 148 Saints. They were mostly men, with only three women and two children in the group. Little Perry Decker, one of Mary Jane's pupils, was one of the two youngsters who were taken along.

Those left behind were so confident that their leaders were guided by God and so impatient to make their way to the new Zion, that they could not wait to learn whether the first company had found a suitable place. They began to make up companies, ready to leave winter quarters. They had a definite plan of organization. Each group would be made up of a hundred able-bodied men with their women and children. Each hundred would be divided into two companies of fifty men; and each fifty, broken down into five small units of ten men and their dependents.

Since there were, all told, nine women and four children in Eliza Dilworth's family, and only three men—Levi Riter, William Bringhurst and John Dilworth (Lavina's husband was away with the Mormon Battalion), the family had to be split up. Mary Jane was to travel in the "ten" with her sister Ann; her favorite companion, Maria, would go with her mother and the Riters. When they camped, the two girls could meet, and it would not be difficult for small William Riter to slip away and walk with his cousin Caleb.

In mid-June, three such "hundreds" set out. Mary Jane's family were all in one of the units of the "hundred" captained by a prominent church member, Jedediah M. Grant. He was a young man, only thirty-one years old, with a sick wife, a baby and a two-year-old daughter. With this personal worry,

96

the captain also was unlucky in the position his company drew for the trek. They were the "third hundred," scheduled to travel behind the other two. This meant that they had to "eat the dust" of the leading wagons. They must delay each morning until the others had pulled out, and, as a consequence, they always arrived at the night camp grounds far later than those ahead.

Mary Jane was acutely aware of the discomfort and of the dissatisfaction some of the Saints felt at this arrangement. She was cheerful and happy, though, and tried to instill into the children who naturally gravitated around her, a feeling of goodwill and purpose. As they crossed the seemingly endless miles of prairie land, she taught them songs and rhymes and devised games to help pass the hours.

There were enough little ones in her group to give her plenty to do. From Amanda Snow, nine, to tiny Charles Crisman, three, Mary Jane found ten boys and girls who looked to her for amusement. This little flock would surround the girl as they trudged along beside the slow-moving wagons. They sang, chatted and listened to their "teacher" when she told them stories of the experiences and adventures their church leaders had known.

This company left winter quarters on June 17, and, for more than three months of burning summer, they moved slowly westward. From time to time a messenger was sent back from Brigham Young, or they found notes and letters hidden in the bleached buffalo skulls along the way.

So they crossed the plains and by early September they were climbing the slope toward the crest of the Continental

Divide. The whole party was camped on the Sweetwater River, resting for the final ascent, when great excitement ran like a brush fire through the people.

Mary Jane was amusing her little group when word came that President Brigham Young and a party had arrived from Zion on their way back to winter quarters to bring out their families, whom they had left behind. All work ceased as the travelers gathered to hear their beloved leader speak.

Mary Jane picked up the toddler Charles, and with the others scrambled around her, she hurried to join the assembling Saints.

She had no idea of the picture she made, standing at the edge of the crowd, holding up the little boy so he could see President Young with the other children clustered about her skirts. But Brigham Young's shrewd blue eyes missed little, and they rested with obvious pleasure on the group. He finished speaking to his people, answered their questions and and then purposefully strode over to Mary Jane.

"Sister Dilworth," he said, his remarkable memory furnishing her name, "I have a special mission for you. As soon as you reach the city, I want you to start a school for the younger children. Let any who wish to, attend, and encourage all to do so. And God bless you."

It was characteristic of the man that he gave no detailed instructions, and characteristic of the Saints not to ask for any. When one was given a "mission" he was expected to find the ways and means of carrying it on.

On October 2, Mary Jane was walking beside the wagon

98

when it emerged from the canyon east of the "city." She paused in awe and wonder. Before her lay a valley, its tall, wild grasses, underbrush and willows browned by an early frost. A cluster of small houses huddled together under the purple haze that softened the distance where a band of glittering silver marked the Great Salt Lake. Blue mountains rimmed the valley, giving it the aspect of seclusion and safety. This was their new home. This was Zion, to which all Saints would be gathered.

The spell was broken as music filled the air and a brass band came marching toward them, surrounded by eager Saints. Welcomed as heroes, the newcomers greeted friends and relatives, and, singing with joy, they went down the slope and across the plain to the waiting city.

It was truly a city, Mary Jane found, though the houses were small. They were set along well-marked streets running due north and south or east and west. At the western border, a fort had been formed by the rear walls of the cabins. These were built close together with the roofs sloping inward to make a strong enclosure, with an open square in the center. It was to this "fort" that Mary Jane's family came. They would live in their wagon, as they had done these past months, until a cabin could be built for them.

Two weeks and three days after the travelers arrived, on October 19, the bell from the Nauvoo Temple rang out, summoning children to the first school in the area that would later be Utah.

Mary Jane had been busy during those two weeks. She had

found someone to set up a conical army tent in one corner of the Square. She had helped others fashion benches from short lengths of logs, which could not be used in the building of cabins. Her desk was the seat from a wagon. She had gone through the settlement collecting books that she could use in classes. She had not had much success, but she had found an old blue-backed speller, a couple of Lindley-Murray readers and a copy of an old arithmetic book, which, the donor explained, had been the first arithmetic written by an American for use in the United States. It was further enhanced by having been recommended by George Washington.

Nine children gathered before the tent. Mary Jane, trying to look businesslike in her gray calico, appeared. She looked over the scrubbed, bright faces and silently prayed that she might serve them well.

"Come, children," she said. "Come, we will begin now." She led them into the make-shift school room, assigned a place to each of them and opened the day's work with a prayer and a hymn.

Reading, writing and arithmetic were the main subjects taught in that first school. There was a great deal of reading and memorizing from the Bible; lots of drill in spelling with spelling bees to which parents were invited. There was work on the times tables. Mary Jane taught with many drills in the belief that what the children learned thoroughly they would never forget. She loved teaching and, as long as she lived, she would always be ready to teach either a whole class or an individual child.

Mary Jane had turned sixteen on July 29, while she was on her way to the West. At the dances in the Fort that winter, she met young Francis Asbury Hammond, whom she married on November 11, 1848, when she was only a few months past seventeen. In the summer of 1851, her husband was sent as a missionary of the Mormon Church to the Hawaiian Islands, which at that time were called the Sandwich Islands. With her baby in her arms, Mary Jane accompanied Francis on this mission. During the six years in the Islands, she taught at a school for the young islanders, as well as "mothering" the unmarried Mormon missionaries—cooking and sewing for them.

She and her husband finally settled in Huntsville, in northern Utah, where again Mary Jane taught school. She died June 6, 1877, just before she turned forty-six years old.

Mary Jane's grave was the first one in the cemetery of that small town. It is marked by a granite shaft bearing the inscription

IN HONOR
OF
The First School Teacher of Utah
Mrs. Mary Jane Dilworth Hammond

Today, the Mary Jane Dilworth school is a fine, modern elementary school in Salt Lake City. It is a still more suitable monument to the young girl who was never too busy with her own affairs to give time to the teaching of young people.

CHAPTER SIX

SEARCH FOR TWO SISTERS
Lorenzo Oatman (1837–1900?) and the Indian Troubles of the Southwest

In spite of bone-aching weariness, fourteen-year-old Lorenzo Oatman could not get to sleep. His blankets were soaked by the drizzling rain. Around him his parents, brothers and sisters seemed to have forgotten their misery in sleep. Lorenzo pulled his covering close to his chin and tried to force sleep to come.

It wasn't only the hunger, thirst and hard work that

103

troubled him. It wasn't even the loneliness of the long journey the solitary family was making across the barren Southwest. More than any thing else, he worried about his father. The boy shivered, remembering how his father had changed during the past days.

That evening, sitting beside the fire of wet greasewood, his empty bowl on his knees, the man had wept openly, like a child. Lorenzo couldn't bear to watch. It was so unlike Royse Oatman to show any sign of weakness or discouragement. He was a truly brave man; he had shown no fear of setting out alone with his family; he had no terror of the hostile Indians which were said to infest the area. But hardship had sapped not only his physical strength, but his courage as well. Lorenzo knew that, as the eldest son, he must assume a good deal of the responsibility for the family's welfare.

Sleep came at last to the boy, but his dreams were riddled with pictures of the past. Some were pleasantly warm and inviting: their home on an Illinois farm before his father had injured himself by lifting a heavy load; the journey to Missouri through a green countryside, where friendly settlers welcomed them and listened avidly to the news they brought. Even the rendezvous at Independence, with the party that planned to make the trip West with them, had been filled with excitement and joy.

They had left Independence in high spirits last August, but, before long, disagreements had ruptured the good feeling. The boy moaned as his subconscious relived the scenes of resentment and anger; of disputes over the best trail to follow; of some wagons turning away; of his father with twenty others starting again with eight wagons to follow their predetermined trail.

That had been the first breakup. After that, first one and then another had set out on a vague, uncharted trail until only three families were left together, the Wilders, the Kellys and the Oatmans. And then, just a week before, the Wilders and Kellys had decided to go no farther. They would spend the spring with some friendly Pima Indians, waiting for the end of the rains that would certainly hinder them on the way. But Royse Oatman had refused to linger. It was already March and he hoped to get to his new location in time to do some spring planting. So the Oatmans had set out alone.

It had been a slow and difficult journey through sand wetted by the spring downpours, across swollen rivers and over slick mountain paths that could not be called roads. Their food had disappeared, until their mother had put them all on strict rations. The two cows were giving no milk, and the gaunt oxen were so weak they could scarcely draw the heavy wagon. All the children had had to walk. Even the two-year-old baby had trudged manfully along through the heavy sand. When the short legs had given out, Lorenzo had carried the little fellow piggyback.

Finally, they were camped for the night on a little sandy island in the muddy Gila River with their food almost gone and blankets soaked.

Lorenzo awakened to the sound of his father chopping wood. He leaped up from his wet blankets and ran to help.

105

Shivering in the gray morning air, he was glad for the exercise to warm his chilled muscles. It took some time, but they finally got a fire blazing. The rest of the family woke up and came to crowd around the flames.

Lorenzo studied them, wondering how they would stand up to the day's ordeal. His mother's face, tanned and toughened by the desert winds, was sad, though she tried to smile cheerfully as she snuggled the two-year-old in her arms. His oldest sister, sixteen-year-old Lucy, was stirring some herbs and wild grass in the pot of boiling water. Twelve-year-old Olive and seven-year-old Mary Ann were trying to comfort small Royse and the littlest sister. Lorenzo sighed. Royse was his nearest male helper—and he was a baby still, just five years old.

Lorenzo hastily swallowed his portion of the tasteless, weak soup and went to hitch up the oxen. His mother and sisters packed the few utensils they had used. They spread the wet blankets across the wagon top, hoping the sun would come out and dry them.

They forded the river in silence and started up the wet road. Lorenzo, with the baby on his back, walked beside the ox team, goading it on. His father trudged beside him, but they did not talk. Thus the sad little caravan proceeded, making only a few miles that morning of March 19, 1851. It was nearly noon when they came to the foot of a steep hill. The oxen turned weary eyes upward, stopped in their tracks and refused to move. Fortunately, the rain had stopped and the sun was shining.

"We'll have to unload the wagon," Lorenzo's father said resignedly. "We can carry everything to the top. I'm sure the oxen will be able to take the empty wagon up."

He unyoked the animals and led them aside to where they could pull off a few mouthfuls of scanty grass. All the others set to work, knowing just what to do for they had met such difficulties before. Mrs. Oatman climbed up into the wagon and handed down boxes and bundles, blankets and utensils. Each child took whatever he could carry and trudged up the hill with the burden. When that was deposited, they hurried back down for another load. To Lorenzo and his father fell the task of taking up the heavier objects—the chests and trunks packed with the things which Mary Oatman felt could not be left behind.

All afternoon they worked, and it was nearing sunset before Lorenzo was urging the oxen to do their share and drag the empty wagon to the summit. The brief rest and scanty fodder had restored some of their lost energy, and they managed to get to the crest of the hill. There the work of repacking began.

Lorenzo's mother was stowing away the articles as the children handed them to her. The boy and his father heaved up the heavier objects. As Lorenzo turned away for a moment, his eye caught sight of something moving on the road below. He squinted down at it and saw that it was a band of Indians.

"Pa!" he whispered, "Indians!"

Royse Oatman whirled. "Yes, but don't be scared, son. You know what I've always said, and I've found it to be true.

Treat them kindly, but firmly, and they'll not molest you."

Lorenzo was not convinced. These Indians, he could see now, were not like any they had met before. They were almost naked, with only a bit of bark or scraggly fur for covering. Their hair hung unbraided.

"Go on with your work, son," Royse Oatman said. "I'll handle them."

Lorenzo obeyed, setting an example for the other children. But they were frightened. Little Royse stood behind the wagon, his eyes wide with fear. Lucy handed the baby up to her mother and then, following Lorenzo's example, she, too, went on with the task of reloading.

The Indians came close. Lorenzo counted them swiftly. Nineteen! All of them were armed with bows and arrows and war clubs. These were no friendly Pimas! His father stepped forward, raising his hand in the universal gesture of good-will.

The Indians returned the salute.

"Buenas tardes, amigos!" Royse Oatman said, hoping these Indians understood Spanish.

One, who appeared to be the leader, nodded and grunted. "Tabac!" he demanded.

Oatman took his pipe from his pocket and filled it with tobacco. He took one whiff and then passed it on to the Indians. One by one the Indians took a puff on the pipe. Lorenzo felt a release of tension. Smoking like that signified friendliness.

But the next demand sent a shiver down the boy's spine.

108

"Carne!"

Meat! They had no meat with which to answer that grunted order.

"Carne!" the fellow repeated angrily. Then, *"Pan!"*

Royse Oatman shook his head. "We have no meat; no bread!"

If the Indians did not understand the words, they did the tone and the gesture. They began to talk angrily among themselves. The Oatmans hastened with the reloading of the wagon. Perhaps they could get away.

Firmly, quietly, Lorenzo's father repeated that there was no food in the wagon. "My family is starving," he said. "I cannot take what little food they have and give it to you."

The leader of the Indians spoke to his men. They withdrew a little, arguing among themselves. The Oatmans worked feverishly. The father waited, not daring to turn his back.

Suddenly, with a wild yell, the whole group rushed upon the Oatmans, clubs raised. Attacking the father first, they battered him to the ground. One fellow grabbed Olive and another dragged Mary Ann to one side. Lorenzo leaped to protect his sisters. A club smashed him to the ground. He tried to rise and was beaten down again. Through blood and tears he saw Lucy fall and his little sister. He heard his mother scream, and then he lost consciousness.

Dimly, through the mists of pain, Lorenzo felt his clothing being torn from him. He felt himself dragged over rocky ground; he thought or dreamed that he was picked up and flung into a chasm. He thought he was falling, but he had no

109

power to scream or to try to save himself. He hit the ground with a thud, and again all went black and still.

A noonday sun beating down upon him awakened the boy. His head was throbbing; every bone and muscle screamed with pain. He tried to open his eyes, but the lids would not lift. He lay there, hurting, trying to remember what had happened. His hands went to his face, fumbled, felt the clotted blood that sealed his eyes, felt the shreds of his torn scalp. After a time he gained enough strength to rub the dried blood from his eyes. Then he could look about him.

He lay on a rocky ledge, with the ground sloping steeply down below him. His outer clothing was gone; his underwear was in shreds. His body was covered with scratches, bruises and dried blood. A trail of blood from the hill's crest above him, told him how he had come to this spot. He lay in the sun and tried to reconstruct what had happened. Evidently the Indians had thrown him down here, thinking him dead. Were any of the others still alive? How could they be? But he must find out.

The top of the hill was only a few sloping feet above him, but he felt he could never climb that far. Dizzy with pain and weak from loss of blood, he started up it. The effort was too much. He fainted, but did not roll back down the slope. When consciousness returned, he started up again.

At last he managed to scramble over the last hump, only to behold a scene of such horror that he felt as if he would faint again. The wagon was overturned, its contents strewn about in wild confusion. Among the goods which the at-

110

tackers had evidently not wanted, lay the bodies of his family
—his father with his head crushed to a pulp; his mother, with
the murdered little boy in her arms; Lucy, recognizable only
by her clothing; his three-year-old sister and small Royse,
both terribly mutilated. Olive and Mary Ann! Where were
they?

Shaking with nausea, Lorenzo crawled around among the
grisly remnants of his family, but he could find no sign of
his two sisters. Slowly he remembered how he had seen them
dragged aside by two of the attackers. He lay down, buried
his face in his hands and wept. Olive and Mary Ann! They
must have been taken as prisoners.

All the boy wanted was to escape from this terrible place.
He began to crawl along the edge of the hill, down the slope
to the road where he had walked the day before. He was unable to stand, so he crept along on his hands and knees to the
road at the edge of the river. Beside the Gila, muddy as it
was, he lay stretched over the edge and drank the thick water.
Then he bathed his blood-coated face and splashed water
over his bruised and aching body. That done, he rolled over
on the bank and slept.

He awoke sometime in the night, with a bright moon shining. He found a stout stick, and, for the first time, managed
to get to his feet. He stumbled along, supported by the stick,
and followed the river until he came to a bluff that blocked
his way. Two days ago—was it only that?—the wagon had
crossed the river at this point. Lorenzo stared at the muddy
current and knew he could never cross it. He turned to study

111

the bluff. It, too, seemed impossible, but he gritted his teeth and started up. Somehow he managed to reach the top and to make his way down again to the road.

All night long he stumbled on, and, when the sun rose, he did not stop, but crawled doggedly forward. He needed water more than anything else. About midday he came to a muddy pool, drank and dropped to sleep beside it. He awoke after awhile and tried to go on, but the afternoon sun was hot and his strength failed. He fell beside the road in a faint.

A strange sound awakened him. It was deep dark now, and the boy sat up, trying to recognize the noise. Then he saw what it was—a pack of coyotes, slavering, yelping, anticipating a good meal. Terror gave him strength. He leaped to his feet, yelling and striking at them with his stick. The beasts drew back, and Lorenzo realized that the yell had been the first sound he'd made since he had fallen under the Indians' clubs. He set out again along the road, with the pack of coyotes following. He dared not stop. Through the darkness he could see their eyes gleaming and smell the odor of their dirty, shaggy bodies. He picked up stones and flung them madly at his tormentors. He was terrified that he might faint again and be torn to shreds by their fangs.

Toward dawn the beasts gave up and slunk away. Lorenzo struggled on until he felt sure he was safe from them. Then, exhausted, he dropped to the ground and slept.

He awoke again when the sun was high overhead. He started on, and after awhile he entered the shadows of a steep-sided canyon. And suddenly, there in his path stood two Pima

112

Indians. They drew their bows and pointed arrows at the apparition that had startled them as much as they had startled the boy. Lorenzo weakly lifted his hand in greeting. They recognized him as one of the family that had stopped in their village. They dismounted and embraced the almost dead boy.

When he made them understand what had happened, they spread their blankets in the shade of a tree, brought him water and gave him some of the ash-baked bread they carried. They made him lie down, wrapped the blankets around him and

told him to sleep. They would ride up to the crest where the massacre had taken place, see what could be done and return for him. Then they would take him back to their village. Gratefully, Lorenzo stretched out and slept.

It was dark when he woke up, and the Pimas had not returned. The boy waited for some time, while misgivings filled his mind. What if the two "friends" had gone to their village to betray him? What if they came back to beat him as those others had done? Tortured by such thoughts, he groped for his stick, and stumbled away through the night. At mid-morning, unable to go farther, he crept under a bush and slept.

The sun on his face wakened him. He sat up and looked around. In the valley below him, a wagon train was approaching. He yelled and waved his stick, and, before long, friendly faces were peering at him and kind voices were asking what had happened. He could scarcely speak for joy. Here were his friends—the Wilders and the Kellys. They gave him food and water and explained that they had decided to proceed, after all. When Lorenzo told of the disaster that had overcome his family, they decided to return to the friendly Pimas and get reenforcements before proceeding into hostile country. The boy was wrapped in blankets, placed in a wagon and taken back to the village. Two of the men decided to ride to the scene of the massacre and bury the bodies of the victims.

He never saw the two Pimas again.

For two weeks at the Pima village, Lorenzo was nursed and fed. Then a party came into the village on their way to Fort Yuma, on the Colorado River. They offered to escort the Wilders and Kellys to that post. Lorenzo was taken along.

He was impatient to get to where he could tell United States soldiers what had happened and enlist their help in searching for his two lost sisters. As soon as the party reached the fort, Lorenzo hunted up the commander, Colonel H. P. Heintzelman, and poured out his story.

"I didn't recognize what band of Indians they were," he confessed, "but they did understand Spanish. Oh, sir! Please send out troops and rescue my sisters! They are so young! I can't bear to think what may happen to them."

The colonel shook his head. "We are just about to move to another post," he explained. "We can't stop to search for them when we have no idea where to look."

Weak as he was, Lorenzo flared up at this. "Sir! They are American girls! This post was established to protect our citizens. You must—"

Several officers in the room nodded. "Let us do something, sir!" they begged.

So the colonel appointed a Captain Davis and a Lieutenant Mowry to lead a small band in search of the captives. What they did and where they looked, Lorenzo was never able to discover, but they returned with no news, in time to go to San Diego with their comrades.

The post physician, Dr. Hewitt, had taken over the care of

115

Lorenzo's injuries. When the troops moved to San Diego, Dr. Hewitt was transferred to San Francisco. He had grown fond of the orphan boy and took him along.

"I know influential people on the Coast," he told the boy. "And there are newspapers there that travel all over the country. We'll set up a cry that will be bound to get some action."

Lorenzo went along, unhappy at leaving the region where he felt the search should be made. In San Francisco, at the doctor's suggestion, Lorenzo visited newspaper offices, told his story and begged for help. It was an interesting story, and many a reporter wrote it up and their newspapers published it.

In the meantime, Lorenzo had to live, and he wanted to earn money with which to finance a real search for his sisters. He went to the gold fields and found work. For three years he labored in the mines, hoarding every penny and repeating his story to everyone who would listen.

The California newspaper stories had reached some sympathetic ears. A carpenter named Grinnell had come to Fort Yuma in 1853. There he received copies of papers carrying Lorenzo's story. He made inquiries and learned of the boy's fruitless efforts to get help from the troops. Mr. Grinnell's sympathy was stirred. He made up his mind to do what he could, and he began questioning every Indian and white trader who came into the post. Had they seen two white girls in any Indian village? For a long time he received no hopeful news.

Lorenzo had not given up hope. He had written letter after letter to the authorities in Washington. He had continued to hound the newspapers. He had worked hard to arouse the

116

sympathy of anyone he thought could help. Still he had heard no word of the girls. But after three years in the mines, he had enough money to set out on his own.

First he went to Los Angeles to inquire of the men who had been sent out from Fort Yuma what they had done and what they had learned. He discovered nothing of value. Then he went to the newspapers in the southern California city and told his story over and over again. He went on to San Diego, trying to get a search party organized. He had no luck there and returned to Los Angeles.

While Lorenzo was frantically appealing for help, the Yuma carpenter's persistence was being rewarded. In January of 1856, he met a friendly Yuma Indian named Francisco.

"You have traveled all over this country; visited every tribe," Grinnell said. "You must have seen something of those white girls. Don't be fooled. We know they are there, somewhere, and when they are found, it will go hard on those who have hidden them. On the other hand, there may be something good in store for anyone who helps to find them."

Francisco grinned. "You talk, talk, talk. If you know they are there, why don't you go and get them?"

Grinnell brought out his thumb-worn copy of a Los Angeles paper. He opened it slowly, and, in his most impressive voice, read aloud the story of the Oatman girls. Then, pretending to be still reading, Grinnell went on to say that a large force was being organized to come into the Yuma region, rescue the girls and punish their abductors.

"And don't think they'll be content with punishing only

117

the ones who stole the girls. They'll get even with every man who helped keep the secret of their whereabouts."

Francisco was impressed. He considered for awhile and then said, "There's only one white girl. The other one died, maybe two years ago. One still lives. She is the wife of Chief Eskeneasy of the Mohaves. He bought her from the Tontos."

Grinnell was excited. This was the first definite word any one had been able to extract about the lost girls.

"How can we get her back?"

"I can do it," the Yuma said. "Give me ransom. I'll bring her in."

"How much? How much goods for ransom?"

Francisco shrugged. "Who knows? Maybe blankets, beads, a couple of horses."

Grinnell could scarcely contain his excitement. He didn't have the ransom goods, himself, but he went out into the town begging for help. They all knew him; knew how hard he had worked to find out about the sisters. Perhaps a feeling of guilt that they had done so little made them more generous. Anyway, the carpenter obtained all he required. He gave the goods to Francisco.

"How long will it take?" he asked.

The Yuma regarded the sun. "In twenty days, when the sun is at the same place where it now is, I shall bring her in."

Besides the ransom goods, the Indian was armed with a letter Grinnell had persuaded the commander of the post to write. The letter said:

118

Francisco, Yuma Indian, bearer of this, goes to the Mohave nation to obtain a white woman there, named Olivia. It is desirable she should come to this post, or send her reasons why she does not wish to come.

Martin Burke, Lt. Col. Commanding
Headquarters, Fort Yuma, Cal. Jan. 27, 1856

Days passed, and those who had contributed the ransom goods began to doubt the wisdom of their act. They felt sure the Yuma had tricked the carpenter, and was now enjoying the wealth he had obtained. But Grinnell had no doubts. He sent word to Lorenzo that his sister had been found, and he should hasten to Fort Yuma to welcome her.

Exactly twenty days after his departure, when the sun was half-way down the western sky, Francisco came riding into the post. He led a horse on which sat a girl, or woman, dressed in Indian clothes, her face tattooed and her hair streaming down her back. The watchers stared. Could this be Olive Oatman?

Francisco brought the woman to Grinnell's shop, where she told the carpenter she did not wish to be seen by others until she had obtained some decent clothing.

"I can't do anything about my face," she said sadly. "I was tattooed as a mark of honor to the chief's wife. It will never come off. Never!"

An officer's wife furnished a dress, and that evening Olive

Oatman was presented to Colonel Burke at his headquarters. Her appearance was greeted with cheers, the boom of cannon and the flash of fireworks. Everyone rejoiced now, forgetting how little they had done to rescue the girl.

Lorenzo did not arrive until a few days later. At first he did not recognize his sister, for she had grown from a 12-year-old girl to a seventeen-year-old woman, and she had suffered much.

After their first embrace, they sat down to talk. It would take days for Olive to tell all that had happened to her and for Lorenzo to recount his efforts at finding her. But he was told at once about little Mary Ann's sufferings and death.

Olive related how she and her sister had been driven, barefoot and naked except for their petticoats, all night long after the massacre, and for several days. Then they had come to a Tonto village, where the girls had been treated as slaves, beaten and starved. In the fall of 1851, a Mohave Chief had seen Olive and wanted her for his wife. He had purchased her from the Tontos, but she would not leave without her sister, so he had bought little Mary Ann, too. He had made the older girl his wife, and, as such, she had been treated well. But the Mohaves had suffered near famine, and little Mary Ann, weakened by hardship and sorrow, had died.

Tears filled Lorenzo's eyes as his sister told how she had insisted that the little girl be buried instead of cremated, according to the Mohave custom.

"Some day, brother, we will go and visit her grave," Olive promised.

120

Lorenzo nodded. "I felt in my heart that you were alive. Oh, if only I could have got help, I might have saved poor little Mary Ann!"

"I thought you were dead," his sister told him. "I looked back and saw them throw you over the cliff. I didn't believe that you could survive."

The reunited brother and sister went to Los Angeles for awhile; then up to Oregon to live with a cousin. Later, they moved to New York, where, it is thought, Lorenzo died about 1900. Olive married a Texan, John B. Fairchild, and died at Sherman, Texas on March 20, 1903.

No monument has been erected to the courage and persistence of the boy who spent years in the search for his sisters. Olive is better remembered. A spring near Oatman, Arizona, is known as Ollie Oatman spring. It is believed that when the first troops were looking for the girls, they were hidden in this place. The site of the massacre is marked by a granite shaft, and the town nearby is named Oatman in honor of the family. In 1857, the Rev. R. B. Stratton wrote a book based on the accounts given him by Olive and Lorenzo. It had 231 pages and sold more than 26,000 copies—a best-seller for that time.

CHAPTER SEVEN

CAMELS TO CALIFORNIA
May Humphreys Stacey (1837–1886)
and the Camel Experiment

May Stacey settled back in his seat with a sigh of relief. He had gotten away at last! Though it was only eight o'clock on a mid-May morning and the sun was bright overhead, May was already a bit tired. He shut his eyes and saw again the party last night. As the train began to move, May dozed.

It had been a gala event. All the wealthy youths of the Quaker town of Chester, Pennsylvania had been on hand to

122

bid him goodby. The girls had been lovely in their satin and *peau de soie* gowns, their powdered faces smiling above lace ruffles and their bright eyes flirting behind their painted fans. May grinned. How the young men envied him! Already at nineteen, he was a brevet lieutenant colonel in Uncle Sam's militia; already setting out on an adventure most of them coveted, but would not dare to undertake.

That's the value of having the right friends, May thought. If his father hadn't been so fond of Edward Fitzgerald Beale, even he, May Humphreys Stacey, wouldn't have been able to wangle this assignment. May, himself, treasured the family's friendship with the former Navy lieutenant. He had for years considered the handsome Beale a hero. As a boy, May had listened enthralled to the man's tales of adventure in the Far West with such famous scouts as Kit Carson. He had exulted when word came that Beale had helped General Stephen W. Kearny win California from Mexico.

Finally, he was going to be closely associated with this idol of his boyhood. He was going to have a part in the most amazing experiment the government had ever undertaken. May was familiar with all the details. He knew how, for years, Jefferson Davis had advocated establishing a camel corps to aid the United States troops in subduing the hostile Indians in the deserts of the Southwest.

Now, as Secretary of War, Mr. Davis had been able to gain an appropriation from Congress for this very purpose. Two years before, two of May's father's friends had been sent to the Near East to purchase the animals. Major Henry C. Wayne and David Dixon Porter had shared the command of

123

that expedition. They had visited Tunis, Malta, Smyrna, Constantinople and other cities, the very names of which set May's heart thumping. They had purchased thirty-three animals, which had arrived in Texas a year earlier.

Porter had been sent back immediately to buy more of the curious animals, and had returned with forty-four. Now all were settled at a Texas ranch, with Major Wayne in charge. But the camels were not to remain there. May's hero, Beale, had been appointed to use the camels in surveying a road from Fort Defiance, New Mexico to the Colorado River. Before starting on this project, Beale had visited his old home in Chester, and May had managed to win a place on his friend's staff.

The train stopped with a jerk, and May opened his eyes. He could scarcely believe it had been an hour since he had left Chester, but he was in Philadelphia already. May took his carpet bag from the overhead rack and went out to the platform. He looked around for old Alex Smith, who was to be his boss until they arrived in Texas, but the man was nowhere to be seen.

May hesitated a moment. He had no authority to act, but he knew that there were supplies to be transferred from the Baltimore Railroad station to the depot of the Pennsylvania Railroad on which he and Smith were to travel to Pittsburgh. He set out on foot to the Baltimore station, where he hunted up the right officials, showed his credentials and obtained the goods. These he had transported to the Pennsylvania depot.

There he found Old Alex rushing about, distracted, trying

to find his assistant. When he learned how May had acted so promptly and efficiently, the old man beamed with satisfaction.

"Young folks don't often know what to do. It's a relief to find a fellow that'll act. I'm goin' to make ye my clerk. Ye go on, doin' what ye see needs to be done. I have too much on my mind, anyhow. I'll be plumb grateful fer someone to help."

May smiled at the old man. "I'll be glad to help, sir. That's why I came on this trip."

May went right to work, seeing that all the supplies were properly addressed to Pittsburgh and from there to the boat that was to take them down to New Orleans. In the afternoon, May had a happy diversion in the arrival of three friends from Chester. Hampden Porter, Joseph Bell and Porter Heap had also persuaded Beale to let them join the expedition. Only a little older than May, they had all been friends from childhood. But as relatives of David Dixon Porter, the newcomers were going more for the adventure than for the work, while May felt he must prove his value by doing anything that needed to be done.

He soon discovered that being Old Alex's clerk was no easy job. While Ham, Joe and Port went sight-seeing or played cards or gossiped, May worked. At Pittsburgh, his three friends went out to see the town, but May was kept busy transferring supplies from the train to the boat.

On the afternoon of May 16, 1857, the *Sir William Wallace* steamboat started downriver. Everyone in the party rejoiced to be on their way and to be leaving Pittsburgh which, May wrote in his journal, was "the meanest place of its size in the U.S."

At Cincinnati, they left the *Sir William Wallace* and transferred to the *Queen of the West*. Again May worked while his friends played. It rained all day and May was soaked to the skin, but he did not complain. In fact, he found that he enjoyed the responsibility of being Old Alex's clerk.

On May 26, the boat arrived at New Orleans, where the group had to wait for a ship to take them out of the channel and across the Gulf of Mexico to Indianola, Texas. Mr. Beale joined the party at New Orleans, and May was relieved to see the man he admired so much and who, he was sure, would show the world what a camel caravan could do.

While they waited, May borrowed Beale's horse and rode into the city to visit his mother's sister. His aunt and cousins were delighted to see this relative from the North, and May enjoyed the visit, the good food and the rest from his strenuous duties.

On the first of June, it rained all day. Again May was soaked as he took charge of the transfer of supplies to the old side-wheeler, which would carry them to their destination.

The gulf was rough. The old ship rocked and creaked, and May felt sure they would all go to the bottom. He had changed to dry clothing, and he lay in his bunk wondering whether he had been wise, after all, to volunteer for this job. But by the time the vessel reached Indianola, the sickness had passed, and May was again able to take charge of unloading the supplies.

There was a great deal of work to be done. The wagons, which had been taken apart for more economical storage on ship, had to be reassembled. The mules had to be harnessed and driven about to give them land legs again after their ship journey. Supplies must be checked as they were unloaded, and then reloaded into the wagons.

When everything was ready, the train set out for the 150 mile journey to the ranch of Major Howard, four miles north of San Antonio. There the camels awaited them. For the first time, May saw wide prairies and felt the sense of awe these vast tracts inspired. But he had little time to indulge in such emotion. Mr. Beale, with the three young men from Chester, had hurried on ahead. May found that he was the only person capable of taking charge of the train. Old Alex and all the teamsters looked to him for decisions. He did not particularly relish working without official status, but the job had to be done.

One night some mules strayed away from the camp. May started the train moving the next morning, and then, with a couple of companions, he set out in search of the lost animals. It was so late when the last one was recovered, that the small party had to hurry on through darkness to catch up with the wagons. May had never done any scouting, but he took the lead, riding ahead of his companions, following by instinct the trail he could not see in the darkness. Everyone was in bed by the time May's party reached camp, but Ab, the Negro cook, took pity on the hungry men. He got up, made a fire and cooked them some supper.

One morning when Mr. Beale was absent and Old Alex was far in the rear, Porter Heap took charge of the wagon train. They came to a steep hill, sloping down into a narrow valley almost filled by a rushing stream. Eight wagons made their way down the slope and across the stream in safety. Porter decided that all could get across and ordered the train to move on. They reached a good camping place and settled down for the night. Then Old Alex rode in with word that two of the wagons had been unable to cross the stream. They were bogged down and could not move.

Porter, like May, had never done any of this sort of work. He did not know what to do. The animals had all been hobbled and turned out to graze. May knew what he would do. He would send men and mules back to help the crippled wagons. But this time it wasn't up to him to make the decision, and Porter did not seem able to determine what should be done. While he hesitated, the two wagons came in. Mr. Beale was with them.

The officer dismounted and strode over to where Porter stood. May saw that the man was very angry as he began to berate Porter for leaving a danger spot before all wagons were safe.

"You have not performed your duty as wagon master, sir!" Beale shouted. "I am disgusted!"

Porter answered, as angry as Beale, "I am not a wagon

128

master, sir! And I did not come on this expedition with any intention of acting as one. I took over because I had to——"

Beale cut him short with angry words. Finally Porter shouted, "Sir, I will not submit to this. I resign my post!" He swung on his heel and left the officer standing there.

Porter did not relent. The next morning he said goodbye to Joe and Ham, mounted his mule and rode back toward the coast. May hated to see his friend go. He felt that Beale had a right to be angry but wished he had handled the affair with more courtesy. May decided that he would never give the officer a chance to give him the kind of dressing down Beale had administered to Porter Heap.

On June 16, the train reached San Antonio. May was delighted with the quaint Spanish air of the city. He gazed at the old church where Bowie, Travis and Davy Crockett fell in the battle for Texas some years before. But again the rain came, and the wet train was hurried through the city to its campground on the far side. May stared in disgust at this uninviting place—a barnyard deep in manure, a corral and two or three huts.

May's willingness to do any job and his knack for doing things right had won Beale's admiration. He invited May to accompany him to Val Verde, where the camels were. There they would have better accommodations than at the campground.

May was just accepting eagerly when Old Alex came up.

"Don't ye take my boy, sir!" the old man said. "I need him worser than ye do, and that's a fact!"

129

Beale frowned. "Too bad, Stacey. But—"

May sighed. For a moment he wished he had not been so willing to help Old Alex. And that night he was miserable as the mosquitoes and horse flies and the stench of the corral kept him awake.

The next morning Old Alex set May to transferring the corn they had brought in the wagons to sacks that could be loaded on the camels' backs, once those animals arrived. He was sent into town to purchase empty whiskey casks in which they could carry water across the desert. May went from inn to tavern, from store to market. Everywhere men were serving and drinking whiskey, but few empty casks could he find. With only half the number needed, he returned late that night to the unpleasant camp.

A few days later, Mr. Beale returned from Val Verde, sixty miles to the northwest of the camp. The camels were being brought down by Joe Bell and Hampden Porter. That evening, as the men sat around the camp fires, they heard the soft music of jingling bells. Everyone leaped to his feet and stared into the twilight. May Stacey never forgot the sight that met his eyes.

Slowly swinging along came the strange, ungainly figures —first one, then two and soon a long line of twenty-five—all moving rhythmically through the shadows. Beside the animals walked their attendants, Greeks and Armenians in their native dress. These men had been uprooted from their homes and brought across the ocean for the sole purpose of tending to the camels.

130

May and his companions had but a moment to savor the exotic spectacle. At the sight and smell of the unfamiliar creatures, the horses and mules panicked. Around and around the corral they dashed, heads up, snorting in terror. May leaped to the enclosure, followed by the others. With all their skill they tried to calm the frightened animals, but it was several hours before peace was restored, and the men could roll into their blankets.

May had brought along a camera and the necessary chemicals to make and develop photographs of the experiment. When the camels were turned in with the horses and mules the next day, he tried to take a picture of the strange scene. He had no success, however, so Mr. Beale engaged a professional photographer to come out from San Antonio to take pictures of the camels. These photographs were to be sent back to Washington so the authorities there could see what was being done.

Mr. Beale instructed May to inform the men about the terminology that had been decided upon. The term "camel" was to be used to designate any of the animals, of whatever kind. The one-humped creatures were to be called Arabian camels; the two-humped, Bactrian camels. The term "dromedary" would be used for the Arabian riding camels.

May learned then about the difficulties Major Wayne had met during the year he held the camels at Val Verde. He had tried to use the animals to carry supplies to their camp, but they had so frightened the people and animals of the city that the officials had complained. To avoid trouble, Major Wayne

had a man walk ahead of the animals, crying "Get out of the way! The camels are coming!"

Many of the people were disdainful of the whole experiment and lost no chance to make fun of the camels and their tenders, and of Major Wayne and Jefferson Davis. One day Major Wayne had heard a man remark that all the brag about what the camels could carry was just lies. The camels couldn't carry as much as an ox.

Major Wayne ordered an attendant to bring out bales of hay. While a crowd watched, two bales weighing 613 pounds

were loaded onto the back of a kneeling camel. The crowd sneered. Major Wayne ordered two more bales loaded onto the beast—1226 pounds!

Someone sneered, "Shucks! They kin put it on his back, but I'll bet he can't get to his feet!"

Major Wayne gave an order. The camel rose and walked easily away.

May, hearing this story, shook his head. "I just hope they perform as well for us!"

A number of army mule skinners had been sent to accompany Beale on his expedition across the Southwest. Now May discovered that these fellows were more trouble than the camels, themselves. When they saw how the mules and horses, to which they were accustomed, were frightened of the camels, the muleteers blamed the strange animals and took out their frustration and spite by beating the offending creatures. Also, the camels had a habit of moaning and groaning while they were being loaded. This angered the men, and brought severe punishment upon the animals. The camel's strange, unpleasant odor was something the army men just could not stand. May had his hands full, day after day, watching over the camels to protect them from the clubs of the men.

Perhaps the camel's worst offense was that it was not a patient animal, like the mule. And it had ways of retaliating for an injury. If too heavy a burden was placed on its back, it refused to rise. If the load was not lightened, the camel would let loose its most terrible weapon—a stream of foul-smelling spit would be sent into its tormentor's face. It was a nauseating, stinging, blinding barrage and never failed to infuriate the recipient. As a last resort, the camel would maul a man, tearing his arm or face with its long, tusk-like incisors.

May rescued one fellow in such an encounter. The man had been beating the camel, who spat into his face. Mad with rage, the muleteer had grabbed a club and began to beat the animal harder. It turned away its head, avoiding the blow. Then with a wild scream of rage, it grabbed its persecutor's arm, raking it from shoulder to wrist. May rushed to the fellow's aid, dragging him away from the angry animal. But the man's arm had to be amputated.

May talked to Mr. Beale, urging him to give the men explicit orders not to mistreat the animals and promising them extreme punishment if they persisted. Beale acted on this advice. He, himself, greatly admired the camels and could not understand the bitter hatred felt by the men.

He described the animals: "they are gentle and patient and will endure the greatest hardship. They carry huge burdens and go for days without water. I consider them far superior to the mule." But all his praise meant nothing to the muleteers.

At first, May Stacey was disappointed in the camels. Twenty-five of the best animals had been selected to make the initial journey. Each one was given a load of 576 pounds, which he should have carried easily. But they had been unused to labor for so long that they had grown lazy. May found the first day of the trip to be a nightmare.

He rose that morning at half-past two in order to awaken the cooks and see that breakfast was ready so they could break camp at dawn. But it took so long to load the camels and to harness the noisy and frightened mules, that they did not start till after eight. It seemed like midday to May. And that day they traveled only sixteen miles.

The next day, May rode ahead to the next town to get some iron plate to mend a wagon. In doing such errands and in hunting strayed animals, the young man often rode twice the distance covered by the wagon train. He loved riding, but he knew very well that, riding alone, he was an excellent target for the arrow or bullet of any hostile Indian along the way.

The train was moving through beautiful country, northwest toward Fort Defiance. But water was scarce and the grass was scanty and parched. Horses and mules had to be fed the corn carried by the camels. These animals, on the other hand, could live on the driest, most meager forage. Gradually, as their flesh hardened with exercise, they picked up speed, and finally were daily outdistancing the mules. May found his admiration for the camels increasing as the dusty miles were covered.

The expedition pushed on, through hot and waterless days; through rain and wind and dust. Sometimes they camped in a tiny Mexican village where the men would slip away to enjoy dancing a fandango. Then May had to scour the village to round up the revelers. Before they entered the Jornado del Muerto, May had every whiskey cask he had purchased filled with water. So they traversed the dreaded sixty-mile stretch without difficulty. It took them more than nine weeks to cover the miles between San Antonio and Fort Defiance. Beale figured they could travel from Fort Defiance to the Colorado River in forty-five or forty-six days.

Mr. Beale had become so enamored of the camels as mounts that he had selected one big dromedary named Seid for his own use. While the expedition waited in camp near Fort Defiance, Beale rode Seid to the fort. There he picked up a contingent of soldiers to accompany him to the California border.

It took the expedition nearly two months, from August 23 to October 18, to make the journey from the Indian village, Zuni, to the Colorado River at the point where the southern tip of Nevada now ends. During those months, May Stacey was given more and more jobs to do. He scouted ahead for water, rode back and forth hunting strayed animals and re-

136

mained in camp after the others had gone on, waiting for delayed or lost members to arrive.

During this time, May kept a daily journal, recording every event of importance, opinions of Beale and others, accounts of encounters along the way. He kept notes of the geography and the weather, of plant and animal life and of the villages they passed. Mr. Beale also kept a journal, and the two records give a detailed story of this unique experiment. May's accounts of his own exploits are put down in a matter-of-fact manner, but they furnish exciting reading.

One time May and his two friends, Hampden Porter and Joseph Bell, volunteered for a dangerous duty. An Indian had stolen a gun from the camp and escaped into the brush. The three young men set out to catch the scamp. They found his trail and followed it till they came upon the fellow with the gun. With him were two companions armed with bows and arrows. All three took "shots" at the boys, but they returned the fire. By clever maneuvering, they managed to capture the thief and a young boy. The third Indian escaped. Triumphantly, they brought their captives into camp. The Indians were kept under guard until the older man led the thirsty travelers to water, then released.

By this time the camels had completely captivated May. He agreed with Beale that "Never was anything so patient and enduring and so little troublesome as this noble animal. They pack their heavy load of corn, of which they never taste a grain; put up with any food offered them without complaint; and are always up with the wagons, and withal so perfectly docile and quiet that they have won the admiration of the whole camp."

As the expedition approached the Colorado, bands of Mohave Indians came out with muskmelons, pumpkins and watermelons to trade for anything they could get. May was annoyed when some of these traders demanded a shirt for a melon. However, he was hungry for fresh fruit and vegetables and so met the demand.

They camped beside the river and made preparations to cross. First, they inflated the rubber boat Mr. Beale had brought for this very purpose. In it they could ferry the instruments, papers and supplies across the river.

Their biggest problem was the camels. May didn't think they could swim, but he led a couple of the best animals to the river bank and watched anxiously to see what would happen. The camels stepped into the water and easily swam across to the other side. A loud hurrah went up from the men. Then the rest were hitched together, tandem style, and all swam across.

No one expected trouble with the mules and horses, but these animals did not do as well as the camels had done. Ten mules and two horses were lost in the swirling waters.

At the Colorado, the official survey ended. May Stacey's job was done. Mr. Beale would send his report to Washington, but first he wanted to go to his Tejon Ranch, near what is now Bakersfield, California. May went with him. He stayed there several weeks and then went on to San Francisco. There he took a ship around South America, through the Straits of

Magellan and up the Atlantic to Philadelphia. From there he was soon back home in Chester.

Through his friendship with Edward F. Beale, or through the many newspaper stories, May probably was kept informed of the final chapter in the story of Uncle Sam's camels. Some of these remained in the Southwest, carrying supplies to the various forts for some time. Others were sold to circuses or zoos. Some went to Nevada to carry salt from the wells in the northeastern part of the state to the silver mines at Virginia City. Some, it is said, were transported to Alaska. For many, many years tales came out of the Arizona desert of phantom camels with ghostly riders.

Largely as a reward for the work he had done as a youth of nineteen, May Humphreys Stacey was given a commission in the United States Navy. His first assignment was on the U.S.S. *Crusader*, which was engaged in intercepting the ships of slave traders in the West Indies.

During the Civil War, May became an officer in the U. S. Army. He performed distinguished service at the battles of the Second Bull Run, Antietam and Fredericksburg. He was awarded several honors for his Civil War service. He continued in the army after the war was over. When he died on February 12, 1886, he was forty-eight years old.

May Humphreys Stacey was one of the almost-forgotten heroes of American history. Scarcely anything, today, preserves his name to attract the interest of young people. His journal has been published and may be found in many libraries. Mr. Beale named a spring at the base of the San

Francisco Mountains, near where Flagstaff, Arizona now stands, Stacey's Spring, but the name does not appear on today's maps. The highest point in Arizona is called Humphreys Peak, but whether for May or for some one else is not recorded.

CHAPTER EIGHT

RIDER ON THE WIND
William F. Cody (1846–1917)
and the Pony Express

Eleven-year-old Billy Cody knew better than to crowd in among the teamsters who were discussing their coming trip to the West. He could hear enough and see enough standing back, ears alert, brown eyes wide and observant. What he heard made the blood race in his veins.

This was his big chance! This was real! He wouldn't just

ride back and forth as a messenger between wagons, here in Kansas Territory or herd extra horses around Fort Leavenworth. This train was going to carry supplies to Col. Albert Sidney Johnston's troops, who were up north, fighting the Mormons. He, Billy Cody, was going to be helping Uncle Sam.

Billy knew quite a bit about the Mormons. He had seen the white-topped wagons winding past on the road in front of his father's cabin in Salt Valley, just a few miles north of the fort. He had heard talks about their strange new religion and of the city they had built out in the desert beside a lake so salty that birds died just flying over it. Folks said they had set up their own government, and now Uncle Sam was sending out his troops to make them obey the laws of the country.

Lew Simpson, big, bluff and given to rough talk, turned and saw the listening boy.

"Hey, you, Billy! Yore to be my helper! What d'ye think of that?"

The boy's freckled face broke into a wide smile—a smile that few adults could resist. "I'd be plumb tickled, sir!"

Simpson chuckled. As the son-in-law of Alexander Majors, their employer, he would be wagon boss. Billy knew it would do no harm to be under his special care.

"Wal, we roll tomorrow. You be here an' ready, Billy. Yore goin' to see real action. Somethin' ye kin tell yore kids about some day."

Billy's pulses quickened. All his life his family had told him that he was destined to be famous. Even before he was

142

born, a fortune teller had predicted that his mother would have a son who might one day be President of the United States. He hadn't had a chance to do much yet, but this might be the beginning of his career.

The next morning he was on his little gray mule, waiting, when the cry, "Ro—o—ll o-u-t!" set the long wagon train snaking forward. This was nothing new to the boy, except that the train was longer and was going farther than any he had worked with before. He felt he was a seasoned bull-whacker, as the teamsters were called, having worked for more than a year now for Alexander Majors, head of the famous freighting company that had undertaken to carry supplies to Uncle Sam's troops. But even before his first job, Billy had played a small part in the history of the frontier.

He had been born in Iowa on February 26, 1846, the son of Isaac and Mary Cody. When Billy was seven, his father had loaded his family into a fancy carriage and taken them, with all his animals and goods, to take up a homestead in Kansas Territory. Coming from the North, Isaac hated slavery, and one evening he had expressed his views to a crowd of settlers from Missouri. These people were determined to have slavery in Kansas, and they had resented Isaac Cody's remarks.

In the ensuing tussle, a hoodlum had stabbed Billy's father. The wound was serious, but not fatal. Billy, young as he was, had helped rescue his father and had hidden him in a field till the danger was past. After that, the northerners had little peace, and the small boy had learned many a trick to put the "abolitionist haters" off the track. At one time he had made a desperate ride past ambushed enemies to warn his father of danger lurking along the road. Later, the death of his father had made it necessary for Billy to get a job to help his mother.

During the past year, working for Majors, Billy had spent hours learning the trade of bullwhacker. The teamsters enjoyed teaching the alert youngster. It was a man's job to handle the bull whip, with its hickory handle four feet long and its lash one hundred feet in length. The lash might be tipped with a dynamite cartridge to make a shot-like crack that scared the oxen into a faster pace. For the animals were not struck by the whiplash—it was the crack that startled them into action.

A bullwhacker must be expert in handling this terrifying weapon. Standing with feet wide apart, he would twirl the lash above his head in a graceful arc. Then, with a snap of his wrist, he would send the slender black thong out, out over the heads of the dallying animals. As it reached its full length, the "crackers" would explode with a shot-like bark that could send chills down the spine of the uninitiated.

Billy was tall for his age, but slender. His wrist bones were scarcely larger than the whiplash. Yet, by diligent practice, he developed the muscle, strength and skill to handle a bull whip as expertly as most of the men.

There were other skills the boy wanted to acquire. He had been ashamed when he had been unable to write his name for Mr. Majors. So, during the long evenings beside the campfire, he would take a charred stick and practice writing the letters shown him by a friendly teamster. He also practiced shooting, both with a gun and a bow and arrow, throwing a lance and riding bareback. His education in these skills had begun when, at the age of seven, his father had given him a pony. He had ridden out to the Kickapoo Indian reservation near his home and had made friends with the Indian boys, who had let him join their games and sports. Commanding all these skills, the tall boy felt that he was equal to any emergency.

That there might be danger along the way was the talk of the men. Trouble did come on Billy's first short trip a year before. What had happened was never actually recorded, but the story went that Indians had attacked the train. Billy had stood his ground like a man and had actually killed his first Indian in the skirmish. Years later, the grown-up William F. Cody recalled that the newspapers had seized upon this account and had labeled him the "youngest Indian fighter on the plains."

However that may have been, afterward Billy was accepted as a full-fledged teamster, equal to any demand made upon him. One day, while they were still crossing the Kansas prairies, he had a chance to show his mettle.

The wagons had just rolled out at dawn, when a sound like thunder shook the air; the earth trembled, a cloud of dust came tumbling toward them. Before the startled men knew what was happening, a great herd of buffaloes came pounding down upon them. The great, shaggy beasts evidently had been stampeded by Indians or by careless white hunters. There was no time for escape. The brown avalanche came straight toward the slow-moving wagons.

The oxen were terrified. In their panic they dashed helter-skelter, desperate to avoid the oncoming horde. Wagon tongues snapped; wagons overturned; the precious cargo was scattered as the scared animals, bellowing, dashed this way and that.

It was Billy's first encounter with the shaggy King of the Plains. He grasped his gun, thinking he would become a hero by killing a fat calf. But he was so excited that his hand shook and he was unable to aim. At the same time his little gray mule, deciding the oxen were wise to get out of the way, lifted its head, snorted and galloped toward the distant hills.

When the boy finally got control of his mount and returned to his companions, he found the men busy salvaging supplies, mending wagons and "making meat" from the buffalo brought down by calmer marksmen than he had been. There was some good-natured joking about Billy's first buffalo "hunt," but before long all this was forgotten.

They had proceeded half-way across southern Nebraska when another danger threatened. This time it was neither Indians nor buffalo, but a group of Mormons sent out by Brigham Young to impede and harass the threatening troops. They had been told to do anything they could to prevent the soldiers from entering the city, which had been evacuated by all but a few men who had been left behind to burn it to the ground if the troops should come.

As Lew Simpson's train entered a narrow defile, now known as Simpson's Hollow, a band of bearded and armed men rode out of the hills and surrounded the wagons. The leader barked orders, and the bullwhackers were immediately

146

disarmed. They did not recognize the leader of the band, for the name of Lot Smith had not yet become known as the scourge of Johnston's army.

"Where is your captain?" Smith asked.

He was told that Simpson was out hunting some cattle which had strayed. Leaving a guard around the train, Smith rode out to meet the wagon boss. They met about half a mile from the train.

"Hand over your pistols!" Smith demanded.

But Lew Simpson wasn't one to respond quietly to such an order.

"No man ever took them from me yet!" he snarled. "And if you think you can do it without killing me, try it!"

Lot Smith regarded the angry man. "I admire a brave man," he said, "but I don't like blood and my orders are to injure no man. I could kill you in a minute, but I don't want to do it."

They were riding side by side, the noses of their horses almost touching. When they reached the train, Simpson saw that his men were disarmed and under guard. There was nothing to do but surrender.

Billy Cody was watching all that went on, more curious than frightened at the sight of these people who had, he thought, challenged the might of the United States Government. Then the Mormon asked Simpson what would happen if he returned the guns to the teamsters. Simpson answered, "We'd fight you to the death!" Lot Smith chuckled.

In the end, Smith gave the freighters two wagons loaded

147

with provisions and sent them on their way westward. As he
rode along with the unhappy men, Billy looked back and
saw the proud Conestogas burning fiercely. The canvas tops,
all aflame, fluttered in the breeze as thousands of dollars worth
of supplies and scores of wagons made a huge bonfire on the
prairie.

Thus, before he even reached his teens, Billy Cody took
part in one of the exciting chapters of western history. He did

not understand what was involved in the struggle against the Church of Jesus Christ of Latter-day Saints (whom he knew only as Mormons) and the United States Government. All he knew was that, here on the prairie, a fortune in goods was being destroyed.

Lew Simpson led his depleted train on to Fort Bridger. When they discovered that this post had been taken over by the Mormons, they detoured and went into winter camp nearby. During the following long months, Billy learned

about life at a true frontier post. When spring came, Johnston's army marched on to Salt Lake City, and the hungry, weary teamsters returned to Fort Leavenworth.

On their way they had a dangerous encounter with a band of hostile Indians, during which young Billy, now thirteen, stood staunchly beside Lew Simpson, using his gun as directed by his boss.

Once back at Fort Leavenworth, Billy drew his wages and hurried home to hand the shining dollars to his mother. He found her in poor health, running a tiny "hotel" in Salt Valley. She had incurred many debts, which Billy's wages only partly satisfied. She hated to have her son leave again, but money was desperately needed, so she let him return to the freighting company. There he easily obtained employment again.

For the next two years Billy Cody worked at men's jobs— as a teamster during the summer and as a trapper through the long winter months. Deciding he could never get rich at such jobs, he went with two companions to the newly discovered gold diggings at Cherry Creek in western Kansas Territory (now Colorado). They arrived too late to reap any golden harvest, and disillusioned, started back home again.

It was the spring of 1860. Billy Cody was fourteen years old, a tall, lithe youngster who was absolutely at ease on horseback, an excellent shot, an experienced bullwhacker and wise in the ways of living on the plains. For three years he had been working on his own, often drawing a man's wages. Always ahead of him glimmered the idea that some

150

day he would be famous, as the fortune teller had predicted. So far he had been able only to do the task at hand. That spring, he looked about him for a better job than he had so far had.

About that time, his old employer, Alexander Majors, had joined with two other businessmen to form the company of Russell, Majors and Waddell. They had decided to undertake a new and daring project—a Pony Express.

The gold rush to California eleven years earlier had sparked the settlement of areas along the Pacific Coast. The Mormons had established many bustling, thriving communities between the Rockies and the Sierra Nevadas. The threat of a civil war darkened the horizon. Political parties were jockeying for position. Abraham Lincoln and Stephen A. Douglas were carrying on their famous debates. It was unthinkable that all the settlers in the Far West should be kept in ignorance of what was happening, or learn of events weeks after they had occurred.

Stimulated by the situation and by visions of serving the country, while at the same time they reaped a fortune, the new company hit upon their scheme. They would purchase the fastest horses, employ the hardiest riders and send mail and news across the country on flying hoofs. Already the telegraph and the railroad had reached St. Joseph, Missouri. From this point to the Pacific, the partners declared, mail could travel in just ten days instead of taking more than a month.

The plan was to have a "change" station every fifteen miles

151

or so along the entire route. At these stations a fresh horse would be saddled and waiting for the rider. "Home" stations were to be established about seventy-five miles apart. There the rider would hand his pack over to a fresh man, rest for a night and return over the same route the following day with his new load of mail.

The riders had to be lightweight—none over 125 pounds. They needed to be tough enough to stand the gruelling hours in the saddle, through all sorts of country and all sorts of weather. They had to brave the dangers of hostile Indians, wild beasts or highwaymen. Above all, they needed to be so loyal to the company and to their jobs that nothing would turn them aside from carrying out their run.

The first Pony Express rider, John W. "Billy" Richardson, left St. Joseph at 7:15 P.M. on April 3, 1860. The first run to San Francisco was made in nine days, twenty-three hours —one hour less than scheduled. At the same time, riders were galloping from San Francisco to St. Joseph.

It was inevitable that such a romantic job would appeal to young Billy Cody.

During his wanderings, he had met an old teamster, George Chrisman, who became the agent for Russell, Majors and Waddell at Julesburg, in the northcentral Kansas Territory. Billy asked for a job as Pony Express rider. The company had planned to employ only riders between the ages of eighteen and twenty-one, but had stretched the requirement a bit to engage some older and some younger riders. Still, a boy of fourteen was something to be carefully considered.

152

Chrisman knew Billy. He knew that the boy had been working like a man for several years and had always performed in a resolute and trustworthy manner. He decided to give the youth a chance and engaged him to act as a substitute rider over a short run of forty-five miles. He would have three hours to make the run, with three changes of mounts. He would be used only in emergencies. He could begin at once, as the regular rider was absent.

For several weeks Billy enjoyed the gruelling, but romantic job as the youngest Pony Express rider ever employed. Then the regular rider returned and the boy was again out of work. For a time he wandered about the area, picking up odd jobs. Then, in mid-summer, he was back at Julesburg, where now J. A. Slade, called Alf, was the agent for the express company.

Slade was one of those characters who are said to be a good friend but a terrible enemy. He was tough and cruel. It is said that he wore an enemy's ears as a watch charm. His reputation varied between loyal employe and outlaw. But he was attracted to Billy Cody, and, when he learned that the boy had already had some experience, Slade put him on the payroll as a regular rider.

It was a proud moment for the youth when he could sign his name at the bottom of the oath required of all riders:

I, William F. Cody, do hereby swear before the great and living God that during my engagement, and while I am an employe of Russell, Majors and

Waddell, I will under no circumstances use profane language; that I will drink no intoxicating liquor; that I will not quarrel or fight with any other employe of the firm; and that in every respect I will conduct myself honestly, be faithful to my duties, and so direct all my acts as to win the confidence of my employers. So help me God!

Billy was not given the easy run he had been assigned before. He was to carry the mail over seventy-six miles of rough country from Red Butte on the Platte River to Three Crossings on the Sweetwater, in what is now Wyoming. It was one of the most dangerous sections of the entire route. Hostile Indians, white desperadoes and wild animals infested the rugged hills and the rushy bottoms. Three Crossings was so named because a traveler had to cross the rushing stream three times within a few rods. In places, the canyon was so narrow that the stream filled it from rocky wall to rocky wall. Billy always arrived at the final station tired, wet and hungry on a horse as weary as its rider.

The mail did not get wet. Letters for the "Pony" had to be written on tissue paper, rolled into a pencil-thin tube and wrapped in oiled silk. They were carried in a "mochila." This was a specially designed leather pouch, which was slung across the saddle, hanging down on each side. A padlocked pocket in each corner held the precious mail and dispatches. The mochila had to be changed with each change of horses, and the rider was allowed only two minutes in which to unfasten the pouch and transfer it to the new mount.

Difficult as his run was, Billy enjoyed every minute of it. He was riding, free as the wind, and getting a handsome wage for doing so. He was aware of the dangers but was confident he could handle any that arose. He did. One adventure brought a measure of fame to the boy rider.

Billy rode into Three Crossings one day to find that the station tender had a fresh horse saddled and ready, but the rider who was to meet the boy and carry the mail the next eighty-five miles to Rocky Ridge had been killed in a fight. There was no one to go on. Billy did not hesitate. Wet and weary as he was, he slung his mochila onto the waiting horse, mounted and galloped off to the next station.

At Rocky Ridge the rider from the West waited to take over Billy's mochila and carry it on its westward journey. He handed the boy the eastbound pouch and started on his return trip. Billy had already traveled 161 miles without rest, but he mounted a fresh horse and started back with his new packet of mail. He would have to take it all the way to Red Butte—another 161 miles, and he would have to hurry to get there on schedule.

Twenty-three hours after leaving his home station, he rode in with the mail. He had made a continuous journey of 322 miles at an average speed of more than fifteen miles an hour. This was the longest Pony Express ride ever recorded, and one of the longest rides in all history. To Billy, it was just doing his job.

He had other adventures. Only a few days after his record run, he was chased by a band of Sioux, but his horse was fleet and he outdistanced the Indians.

155

At another time, two road agents attempted to hold him up to rob him of the gold he was reported to be carrying. This time Billy dismounted and pretended to be unfastening the mochila. Suddenly he whirled and threw his blanket into the face of the bandit holding him at gun point. Then, leaping on his mount, he rode right over the befuddled man. The other highwayman came running, but the boy put a bullet through him and rode on, his mochila safe.

About that time, the boy became friends with Wild Bill Hickok, one of the famous characters of the early West. They may have met before, but if so, it was only a passing acquaintance. Finally Billy was man enough to consider himself an associate of the noted character. With Wild Bill, the young Pony Express rider took part in a raid against a hostile Sioux village, whose braves had been stealing horses from the station. There were some forty men in the raiding party, which surprised the Indians, recovered the horses and took some Indian ponies in payment for their trouble.

By autumn of 1860, Billy was no longer riding on a regular run, but was again a "supernumerary" or extra hand. He rode when needed and did extra jobs around the station. Thus he was on hand when the men came in with the exciting news of events out in the world. He heard of the election of Abraham Lincoln as President in 1860. This made a deep impression on the boy—a backwoodsman had achieved this high honor. Perhaps the fortune teller's prediction might yet come true.

In March of 1861, Pony Express riders carried Lincoln's

inaugural address across the West, from St. Joseph to Sacramento in seven days, 17 hours. In April, word that war had been declared between the North and the South flashed by on pounding hoofs.

Romantic as it was and good job that it had done, the Pony Express was doomed. On October 26, 1861, the telegraph wires from East and West were joined at Salt Lake City, and the need for the "Pony" was over.

At fifteen, with the Civil War raging, Billy Cody would have liked to enlist. He strongly remembered his father and the troubles his family had suffered at the hands of "abolition haters." But his mother persuaded him not to try. He did join a band of "jayhawkers"—young Kansas fellows who took it upon themselves to harass and rob the people on nearby Missouri farms. It was plain outlawry, but the youths excused it by saying it would help the North win the war.

Billy's mother was unhappy with her son's activity and tried to get him to leave the outlaw band. Fortunately, Wild Bill Hickok came by as wagon master of a train carrying supplies to the northern troops. He persuaded Billy to join him. Later, Wild Bill got his young friend a chance to scout for the Union Army.

In November of 1863, while the youth was in Denver with a wagon train, he learned that his mother was dying. He hastened home to be with her at the end. The next February he enlisted in the Union Army.

Many stories have been told of young Bill Cody's experiences as a soldier, but few of these have ever been authenticated. He never rose above the rank of private, and it can be assumed that his experiences were just those of most soldiers in the ranks. He visited St. Louis in 1865 and met Louisa Frederica, whom he married in March of 1866. The war was over, and William F. Cody had just turned twenty.

In 1867, young Cody earned the title by which he was to become world famous—Buffalo Bill. He was, at that time, employed by the Kansas-Pacific Railroad to kill buffalo to feed the workmen laying the shining rails across Kansas. For five hundred dollars a month, he was to furnish twelve buffalo a day—an easy task for such a sure shot as Bill Cody.

One time another buffalo hunter, Gen. George A. Custer's favorite guide, Billy Comstock, challenged Cody to a buffalo-killing match. Trains from St. Louis brought crowds out to watch the contest. It ended by Cody killing sixty-nine animals to his opponent's forty-six. Altogether, it is said that Buffalo Bill killed 4,280 of the shaggy animals in eighteen months. Today, this is regarded as a doubtful honor.

William Cody tried many different jobs. He served as an army scout for Generals William T. Sherman, Philip Sheridan, Nelson A. Miles and Custer. He made friends with Indian chiefs of many tribes, though he often fought hostile groups. The Indians gave him his second nickname of Long Hair.

But at last the young man found an occupation which interested him more than any other. He collected a vast aggregation of cowboys, Indians, sharp shooters, horses and wild animals of the West and organized Buffalo Bill's Wild West

158

Show. With this new and spectacular group, he traveled all over the world. Sometimes his troupe appeared in "command performances" before the rulers of Europe. Queen Victoria of England was particularly delighted with the show.

The main attraction was the famous scout, himself. Tall, straight and handsome, with chestnut hair curling on his shoulders and a smartly trimmed goatee, he was the ideal of western manhood. He wore beautifully beaded buckskin clothes with silver ornaments, and he had the courteous manners of a nobleman. He did not fulfill the fortune teller's prediction that he would become the President of the United States, but he was probably the best known American of his time.

For awhile he made a great deal of money. Then troubles

159

came. The show lost its appeal and debts mounted. For years he struggled to make a comeback, but it was no use. Buffalo Bill's day had passed. On January 10, 1917, the old scout died at the home of his younger sister in Denver.

The world paused to pay him homage. His body lay in state in the rotunda of the Capitol at Denver. A long, solemn cortege of cowboys and other admirers filed along the streets behind the hearse that bore his body. Two cowboys led the scout's beautiful white horse, saddled and bridled but riderless, with holstered pistols hanging from the saddle horn.

William F. Cody, Buffalo Bill, is buried at the top of Lookout Mountain near Golden, Colorado, in a grave hewn from solid rock. A museum of western culture, where many mementoes of the scout's life may be seen, is maintained nearby.

In the Big Horn country of Wyoming stands the town of Cody, named for the old scout. His childhood home has been moved from Iowa to the lawn of the railroad depot there. A log cabin replica of Buffalo Bill's ranch house is a museum containing many souvenirs of his Wild West Show. On Main Street stands a statue of the scout on his favorite horse, Smoky. The Irma Hotel was named by Cody for his daughter. On July 4, the Cody rodeo is held in this town. Cody Trail winds below Cody Peak to the eastern entrance of Yellowstone National Park.

CHAPTER NINE

BELLES AND LUMBERJACKS
Flora Pearson (1851–1925)
and the Mercer Girls

"He's here, Mama! Mr. Mercer's here!" fourteen-year-old
Flora Pearson cried, dancing into the kitchen where her mother
stood, arms floured, kneading the dough for the day's baking.

"My goodness!" her mother exclaimed, "and me such a
sight! Tell him I'll be there in a minute."

Flora hurried back to the parlor of the pretty little house

161

in Lowell, Massachusetts. She explained to the tall, red-haired man that her mother would be delayed a moment.

"But you have letters from Papa, don't you? And from Georgie? Oh, I can't wait to hear what they write."

"Your father wants you and your mother and brother to come out to Washington Territory with me," Asa Mercer told the girl. His nasal, mid-western twang sounded out of place in that New England cottage, but Flora was not conscious of the oddity.

Mrs. Pearson came into the room, her face beaming, her apron discarded and her hands still damp from their washing.

"Mr. Mercer. I'm so glad to see you again! How is my husband? And my daughter, Georgie?" Her voice trembled.

Asa Mercer stood to greet the woman. His lank six-feet-two frame towered over the plump, smiling woman. Beads of nervous perspiration dotted his forehead under the shock of bright carroty hair. His palm was clammy as he shook hands. He was obviously ill at ease.

"They are both well," he said. "I've brought letters from them." Then, hesitatingly, "I'm so sorry about Josie. She was a wonderful girl—and doing a marvelous job teaching the children on Whidbey Island. She was beloved by all—" He stammered to a stop.

Mrs. Pearson spoke calmly. "Yes, my husband wrote about her heart attack on the way to school, last August. I was distraught at having my eldest daughter die so far from home. That is one reason I wish to go back with you. When I heard that you were coming to Boston and Lowell again to get an-

162

other group of women and girls to go to the Northwest, I made up my mind that I'd return with you. I suppose," her voice shook a little, "I should have gone out last year—"

"When Papa and Georgie and Josie went," Flora put in. "Oh, Mr. Mercer! You don't know how I cried because I couldn't go with them. But Mama has promised that I can go this time. You will take us, won't you?"

Mercer had dug into the tail pockets of his rusty black coat and had withdrawn a small packet of letters. He handed these to Mrs. Pearson. She held them in her hands, looking at them, but not attempting to open them or read their messages.

Her glance went to the man's face. "We have our passage money saved. The house and furniture are sold. We'll be ready whenever you say."

Mercer coughed, a little embarrassed. "I must tell you that —ahem!—I've run into some difficulties. I just don't know when I'll be starting back—"

Both Flora and her mother stared at him in alarm. "Tell us about it," the woman finally said.

Mercer settled himself back in the comfortable chair and began, slowly at first, but gradually speaking rapidly as his anger and frustration lent heat to his voice.

He had taken his first group of eleven girls to Washington Territory the previous year. They became teachers, cooks and seamstresses, filling a dire need in the region where there were so many more men than women. Some already had found husbands among the lumberjacks and other early settlers of the Territory.

163

"My venture was such a success, that I came back this spring, hoping to get a shipload of five hundred girls and women of the same caliber. But I have run into nothing but trouble."

He had counted on help from President Abraham Lincoln, whom he had known. He'd sat on Lincoln's lap when he was a child, listening to his comical stories. And he had thought that, now that the Civil War was over, there'd be surplus ships he could easily obtain. But he had arrived in New York the very morning after Lincoln's assassination. He had found no one in Washington to listen to him. Weeks had passed before he finally was offered a ship—but at a price he could not pay.

"I got that ironed out," he told his enthralled listeners. "A fellow—Ben Holladay—bought the ship and is letting me use it. And I got the five hundred fine, New England women and girls signed up. But then—" He swallowed. Flora was fascinated by the prominent Adam's apple that worked up and down the thin neck.

Her mother took pity on the man's agitation. "I know. I've seen the papers. Those New York reporters don't have much to write about. The way they made fun of you and your project! But why would anyone believe those scurrilous stories? You had the best of references—"

"Governor William Pickering of Washington Territory, Governor John Andrew of your own state, Edward Everett Hale—Yes! I have the best references. They all endorsed my plan. But those stories! More than three-fourths of those who

164

had signed up have withdrawn. However," the pale eyes brightened, "however, Mrs. Pearson, I cannot be turned aside. We need good women in Washington Territory, and I mean to take as many as I can back with me. I shall be so happy to have you and Miss Flora. I'll let you know when to come to New York to board our ship. It's the *Continental!*" he finished proudly.

It was a cold, blustery January day in 1866 when Flora ran gaily up the gangway of the ex-troop ship *Continental*, berthed in New York harbor. Behind her came her brother, Daniel, and her mother. Each lugged along a heavy carpet bag filled with things they would need on the trip. Their chests and boxes had been sent ahead from the hotel where they had spent the last two nights.

Among Flora's things was a small bound notebook and a supply of quill pens and ink, safely bottled. She was going to keep a daily record of the journey. She had already written the introduction explaining Asa Mercer's trials in obtaining a ship and a cargo of girls and women. She had put in how her family had first heard Mercer speak in the Mechanics Hall in Lowell in 1864. Her father, an overseer in one of the town's cotton mills, had been out of work for some time. Because of the Civil War, no raw cotton had been coming North to feed those mills, and many had closed. Daniel Pearson had been captivated by the picture Mercer painted of the wonderful Northwest—with its untouched forests, streams and valleys, all teeming with abundance to be taken by any who came.

His daughters had been equally entranced by the tales of

the handsome men—so plentiful on the Coast and so scarce in New England, where the war had drained away the best of the young men. The upshot was that Daniel Pearson and his two elder daughters had gone out to the new land, where one had died.

All this, Flora had written out as an introduction to her journal. Who knows, she had thought as she scribbled, perhaps some day, maybe a hundred years from now, someone will read this!

She skipped up the gangway, her long skirts swishing about her high shoes, her fur tippet snug around her neck and her velvet bonnet securely tied under her chin. She stepped onto the deck and stopped in dismay.

Pandemonium reigned. Passengers, baggage and crew were huddled everywhere. It looked to Flora as if nothing had been done to the old troop ship since its last soldier had left. She had always heard the term ship-shape and had never imagined a vessel could be so dirty, messy and disorganized.

The passengers had all come aboard early that morning, after a scanty breakfast at the Merchants' Hotel. As the hours came and went, no one seemed to be preparing any luncheon for the shivering, hungry people.

Flora tried to ignore her hunger as she followed her mother fore and aft and back again, down and up and down the steep companionway, hunting the cabin to which they had been assigned. Finally, ahead of her in a crowd of chattering, scolding women, she caught sight of the bright head of Asa Mercer. She pushed her way through the noisy group.

166

"Mr. Mercer! Mr. Mercer! Where is our room?"

The distracted man could not hear her above the hubbub. A neatly dressed young man spoke to her. "What seems to be the trouble, Miss? I'm Roger Conant, a New York reporter. Maybe I can help you."

Flora explained her problem, and the reporter agreed to guide her through the maze of cabins till they found the one assigned to the Pearsons. Flora hunted up her mother and away they went in the wake of the obliging young man. He was as good as his word. They found their cabin, with their bundles and boxes piled in the middle of the floor. The two women thanked Conant and set about putting things in order.

Daniel appeared, complaining of hunger.

"There's to be no meal till evening," Mrs. Pearson explained. "A gong will sound when it's ready."

Flora was as delighted as her brother when the gong finally told them they could eat. All three Pearsons hurried toward the dining room. The entrance was jammed with hungry passengers, all trying to be first into the hall.

Flora stepped aside. "I'll wait my turn, Mama," she said. "I can't push and shove like they're doing."

Finally the passageway emptied, and Flora entered the room. Her mother had found a seat at one of the long tables, but there was no vacant place beside her. In fact, Flora could not see a single empty chair. She made her way to her mother. Mrs. Pearson handed her daughter a hunk of dry bread on which was a bit of fried liver.

"That's all I've been able to get," the woman said. "It

doesn't look very appetizing, but you'd better eat it." Then, as she saw the look on her daughter's face, she said quietly, "I'm sure things will be better, once we all get organized."

At dark, the ship, which had been slowly moving away from the city, was stopped at Staten Island. Flora heard a commotion on deck and rushed to see what was happening. She found a crowd gathered about an angry, gesticulating old man.

"What's the matter?" Flora asked.

Martha Chase, one of the girls from Lowell and a friend of Flora's answered. "He wants Mr. Mercer, but Mr. Mercer has disappeared."

No one seemed to know where the agent could be and the irate man finally left. He was muttering angrily that he must leave the ship. He'd paid passage for himself and his family, he claimed, but Mercer had not permitted his family to board. The old man wanted to get back to New York.

Flora turned to her friend. "Well, I can certainly make the first of my journal interesting. The mysterious disappearance of our leader!"

She stopped. Two men were lifting the hatch of one of the coal holes. Annie Stephens, a fashionable young lady from Baltimore, leaned over the opening and cried, "He's gone, Mr. Mercer. And all the others have gone, too—those men you did not want to see. You can come out now."

A shock of red hair, striped with black coal dust, emerged. Two grimy hands were raised. The crewmen grabbed hold

168

and yanked Mercer from the pit. Flora giggled. Martha explained.

"They've been saying that Mr. Mercer couldn't pay all the bills run up by the passengers while they were waiting in New York. So he thought the best thing was just to hide till the bill collectors and dissatisfied folks got off here. From now on, we should have peace and quiet."

Every evening before going to bed, Flora wrote down the events of the day. She was as seasick as the others that first night out, when a heavy storm scared the passengers and upset their stomachs. Yet she giggled when one of the older women, leaning over the rail and "casting her bread upon the waters," lost her false teeth in the process. After that she was teasingly called "Toothless."

From that very first meal, Flora was unhappy about the food. They all had marvelous appetites, due to the sea air, and there was never enough food to satisfy them. Yet in her journal, Flora suggested that it might be a good thing, after all, because no one was sick after that first evening. Two babies were born during the voyage, and one man was lost overboard.

This accident deeply troubled the girl. She had overheard the fellow arguing with the first mate and had been appalled at the ugly look the officer gave the man as he sent him aloft. As the girl watched, the rope broke under the fellow's weight and he went crashing into the sea. Mercer grabbed a life preserver and threw it to the man who was swimming away from the ship so as not to be sucked under it. A life boat was lowered and seamen manned it. They rowed about on the choppy waves till darkness fell, but the man never was found.

Flora entered into the games and amusements that were devised to lighten the tedium. She knitted socks and sewed shirts which Mercer planned to sell when the ship reached Seattle. She helped "little Miss Stevens" teach the children on board in a little school set up in a life boat. There were eighteen children younger than Flora, and she spent many hours amusing them. Her favorite was four-year-old Elswie Peterson, a golden-haired "cherub" whose antics amused everyone.

Down the Atlantic went the *Continental,* through the Strait of Magellan in a terrible storm, and up the Pacific to San Francisco. But there were stops along the way which delighted the girl. She was young and ready to enjoy any new experience. At Rio de Janeiro, where the ship stopped for several days, the girls enjoyed picnics ashore, visits to the native markets and beach parties, where the girls collected pretty shells along the shore.

They found Lota, Chile, blockaded by Spanish ships. The captain of one of these thought the *Continental* was a man-of-war, come to aid the Chileans. He gave chase, caught up with Mercer's vessel and boarded it. Flora thought the end of the journey had come and that the Spaniards would haul them all off to Spain to perish in dark and filthy cells. But what an adventure that would be! She and Martha put their heads together, considering the advantages and disadvantages of such a conclusion to their voyage.

However, the foreign officers studied the *Continental's*

170

papers and decided that both passengers and crew were harmless. They were allowed to enter the port.

Further adventure awaited them there. The Chileans were determined to persuade some of the girls to remain to teach school in this isolated port. Fabulous offers were made—wonderful salaries, a beautiful home, even marriage. Flora, now fifteen, gay and lively, fully expected some of the older girls to be so attracted that they would "jump ship."

Several of them wanted to and were only kept from carry-

171

ing out their wild scheme by Mr. Mercer. He stood at the gangway, pistol in hand, red hair flying, and threatened to shoot the first Chilean who came aboard to steal one of his passengers. Captain Charles Winsor persuaded the girls to wait till morning, when he promised them they could go ashore if they wished to. During the night, he weighed anchor and set out for the open sea. When the girls awoke next morning, they found themselves far from the tempting offers of the Chilean officers.

When the ship reached San Francisco in April, Flora was amazed and shocked at the attitude of the people of that city. Crowds of men gathered about the girls every time they appeared on the street. Women looked askance at the "Mercer Belles" or tried to "rescue" them from the clutches of Mercer, who had been described in the newspapers as a villain. These stories said Mercer had brought the girls from their homes in order to marry them to the "riff-raff" of Puget Sound.

She was happy when she was placed on a lumber boat with her mother and brother and a dozen other members of the party to make the journey from San Francisco to Seattle. This part of the long journey was sheer pleasure. Her fellow passengers were by now all good friends, and the scenery along the coast was lovely.

At the little wooden dock in Seattle, the Pearsons were met by Flora's father and sister. Daniel Pearson had a skiff waiting to take his family to Whidbey Island, where he had been engaged as light keeper. Georgie was teaching school in the settlement there. So Flora bade her friends farewell, promised to see them often and set out with the reunited family for the cabin her father had built.

Flora was delighted with her new home. All around the cabin rose the forest; the ground was carpeted with lush grass; wild flowers perfumed the air and wild berries were ripe for the picking. She learned that the island had been one of the first areas settled on Puget Sound. There had been some trouble with the Indians. Nine years earlier one of the settlers had been killed by the natives in retaliation for the murder of a chieftain by the whites. But since that time the newcomers and the natives had gotten along peaceably. Indian youths worked for the settlers. One of their chief occupations was manning the canoes that carried the people to Seattle and back.

Flora had hoped that she might obtain a position as a teacher in her new home, but there were not enough children to warrant another school. Her sister, Georgie, was teaching at Coupeville, a few miles from their cabin.

"What can I do?" she demanded. "I didn't come way out here to loaf—to be a burden. There must be something."

Her chance came when her father's assistant left, and the post of assistant light keeper was vacant. Flora applied for the job and was appointed.

For the next twelve years Daniel Pearson maintained his position and was never absent for one night from his responsible post. For ten of these years, Flora helped him. She became known all along that part of the coast for her faithfulness.

Flora's work was especially important as that time, for vessels of every kind were plying the waters of the Sound. There was no lighthouse at Whidbey Island. The light keeper had to see that oil-burning lanterns were lighted and placed on the high rocks to warn seafarers of their danger. There always was danger along this coast. Until the establishment of Life Saving stations, the light keeper and his assistant acted as rescuers, administers of first aid and general protectors of the hundreds who sent their small craft up and down the coast.

In 1876, when she was twenty-five, Flora married William B. Engle, who had come to the island in 1852 as one of the earliest settlers. For almost fifty years she helped her husband on his farm. At one time, when she was past sixty, she wrote an account of the Mercer Expedition for publication in the Washington Historical Quarterly. Her memory, supported by the journal she kept during the historic trip, served to bring to life again this unique experiment in the colonizing of the Pacific Northwest. Her article recorded what had happened to many of the passengers during the fifty years since they had left their homes in Boston, Lowell, New York and Baltimore.

Thus, because a fourteen-year-old girl had the intelligence and perseverance to keep a daily journal, today's students of western history have an accurate account of one fascinating event.

CHAPTER TEN

A LIVING TARGET
Clark Stocking (1840–????)
and the Road Agents

Sixteen-year-old Clark Stocking was riding his scrawny little horse, Blackleg, on a summer day in 1856. They were on a lonely stretch of trail, in the hills near Camponville on the north fork of the Yuba River in central California.

He had been working in the mining camps of the Mother Lode, hoping to pick up a fortune as many had done in the

175

past seven years, but he had had little luck. So he was making his way toward Marysville, where he hoped to find a job, for he needed money.

On the road below Clark, and out of sight of the lone rider, a not unusual drama was taking place. Billy Dobson, a veteran stage driver, was rolling merrily along, high on the seat of the Concord stage that ran from Downeyville to Marysville. He had a full quota of passengers—eight, including two women. But that was not all. In the treasure chest under the driver's seat was a hundred thousand dollars in gold dust, sent down from the mines around Camponville.

Billy Dobson was hoping that the news of the treasure had not gotten out among the general public. There were too many road agents, as robbers were called, in the area. Tom Bell, for one, would love to get his hands on this much "dust." This breed of robbers had developed because some men would rather let others dig for treasure, which they could then acquire by merely waiting beside the road and pointing a gun. Billy Dobson grinned to himself. He knew what he would do if any bandit shouted, "Hands up! Throw down the box!"

Just then the coach rounded a point of rocks and there, standing in the road, were five masked men. Four were on

foot, the leader rode a black horse. All five guns were aimed at Billy's heart.

"Halt!" yelled the leader. "Halt and throw down the box or I'll shoot!"

"Shoot and be damned!" roared Billy. He shook the reins over the backs of the horses, shouted an order and away he went, right through the threatening group. His daring did not go unchallenged. A fusillade of bullets answered him. They spattered against the coach and whizzed through the windows. Billy kept on.

At this moment, Clark rode out of the hills. In a glance he took in the situation. He raised his own gun and fired at the bandits. One fell. Taken completely by surprise at this flank attack, and not knowing that the boy was alone, the masked men picked up their wounded companion and fled into the hills.

Clark did not pursue them. He was only one against five, and he was content that he had scared them away from the stage coach. He gave Blackleg his head and galloped down the road after the vehicle.

He caught up with Billy Dobson at Columbia, where the coach stopped to discharge passengers and take on more treasure for Marysville. There was great confusion around the vehicle. One of the women passengers had been struck by a bandit's bullet and been killed. The other woman had been wounded in the leg, and a male passenger had been hit in the arm.

Clark joined the chattering group. "I know who the leader was," he told Billy Dobson. "His mask dropped and I saw his face. It was that Tom Bell everyone has been looking for."

"Thank 'ee, younker!" Billy said. "Ye came just in the nick of time. That Tom, on his horse, could have caught up with us—and he was pretty mad, I know. So ye might say ye saved us all—"

Clark shook his head. "You'd have got away. But I just couldn't see a hold up and do nothing."

Billy stared at the group, muttering angrily over what had happened.

"These folks don't mind doin' nothing," he said grimly. "I'd go back after Tom Bell, myself, but I've got dust to deliver. But somethin' should be done. He's been a terror long enough now. And we could pin this on him, now we have an eye witness."

Billy's grumbling reached attentive ears. A posse was swiftly formed to go back over the road and into the hills after the notorious road agent and his gang. Clark wanted to join the group, but Billy stopped him.

"We need a treasure guard on this line," he said. "What about yore takin' it on, eh?"

He did not need to explain to the youth that he was offering him the most dangerous job in all the West. Clark knew what he was doing when he stretched out his hand to grasp that of the driver.

"I'm your man," he said briefly.

In that casual manner, sixteen-year-old Clark Stocking became the youngest treasure guard on record.

Before the railroad spanned the continent, and even after that for some years, the gold and silver from the rich mines of

179

the West had to be transported to some place where it could be milled and shaped into coins or bars. Then it could be shipped to the cities of the East. This transfer of valuable "dust" or bullion—gold bricks or silver bars—had to be done by coach.

The California and Nevada mines sent their treasure through Marysville to San Francisco. There, it was placed on ships to carry it around the Horn to New York or Philadelphia. Later, when gold and silver were discovered in Montana, Idaho, South Dakota, Colorado and Utah, it, too, was transported by coach to the nearest railhead for shipment to the Coast.

The roads over which millions of dollars worth of gold and silver were transported were not very good. They had been carved out of mountain sides, or laid along a stream bed, or they crossed miles of empty, sage-covered desert. The fact that such fortunes were being carried along these isolated routes was too tempting to lawless men, and the road agent's trade developed.

The outlaws operated either singly or in small gangs. Their usual practice was to step out from behind a rock or tree, guns ready, as the stage came up. If the driver did not stop at their command, a rain of bullets soon convinced him that it was only good sense to comply. So when he was ordered to throw down the box, he generally did so. If a stage carried passengers, these were then lined up and robbed.

As the problem became unbearable, the stage companies sought ways of circumventing the bandits. One expedient was to hire a treasure guard to ride up on the box beside the driver.

180

With his shotgun across his knees, he could answer the robbers' bullets while the driver whipped his horses on out of danger.

The treasure guard was, of course, the first target of the outlaws' guns. It was "kill the guard or be killed." So this officer had to be a man of exceptional courage, coolness and ability. His very life depended on his skill as a marksman. Clark's coolness, quickness and marksmanship showed Billy Dobson that he was a youth of the right caliber. But when he had time to consider the boy's youth, he tried to withdraw the offer. Clark would not hear of it. Already, in his mind's eye, he was riding high on the box, beside his new-found friend.

All we know of Clark Stocking's adventures as a treasure guard must be gained from brief references here and there in the stories of other men. Unlike Lorenzo Oatman, Clark did not meet someone who would write a best-seller about his experiences. Unlike Flora Pearson, he never kept a daily journal; nor did he settle down, as an old man, to write his own story. But here and there, in the accounts of western events, one catches a glimpse of Clark Stocking, cool and courageous, riding the box with his gun across his knees.

Clark joined Billy Dobson in the summer of 1856, riding the stage that carried passengers and treasure through the rich Mother Lode country. Under the high seat reposed the iron-bound treasure chest; heavy with gold dust on the way down, filled with coin and paper money on the return.

How long he covered that road is not recorded. He may have been there in 1860, when a hundred-pound gold nugget worth $25,000 was found at the Monumental Mine in the Sierra Buttes that loomed above the road.

Both driver and treasure guard were paid in accordance with the amount of treasure they protected and the danger of the route they covered. So, as the California mines began to dwindle, Billy Dobson and his companion moved on to a richer field.

By this time the Comstock Lode in Nevada was beginning to boom. Discovered in the early 1850's by Peter O'Riley and Patrick McLaughlin, this rich silver region had acquired the name of Henry "Pancake" Comstock, who did much to develop it. The region was isolated, far from the facilities needed for handling the ore. The first ore was taken to California by ox teams. Later, roads of a sort were constructed, and the famous Concord stages were used. These stages became the special prey of the road agents.

Between Silver City and Gold Hill there was a narrow defile, scarcely wide enough to permit the passage of a coach or wagon. This was the favorite spot for holdups and here many a coach was lightened of its load. It is said that one driver would not wait for the command, "Throw down the box!" As he approached the defile, he got down into the boot and tossed out the box, whether a road agent was waiting or not.

This was not Billy Dobson. He and Clark took their treasure safely over the mountain and down into California without losing a dollar's worth of the fortunes entrusted to them. Clark, not yet out of his teens, was already famous among those who used the coaches, as well as those who harassed them.

182

Later, when the Montana mines were booming, Clark appeared in Bannack, where he was employed by H. A. Conover to ride guard on the first mail and express route from the mines in that area to Salt Lake City. It was in this area that the notorious Henry Plummer operated.

Plummer had killed a man in Nevada City, California. He was arrested, tried and sentenced to be hanged. Friends persuaded the Governor to pardon him, and he went back to his old trade. After killing another man, he fled to Montana, where he was made sheriff of Bannack. At the same time he was leader of a gang of a hundred road agents, who terrorized the roads, until a vigilante committee caught them and hanged several, including Plummer.

Clark Stocking is said to have ridden with X. Beidler, who won fame in western annals by his fearless attacks on this outlaw gang. That must have been one of Clark's most dangerous periods. From the gold mines in Montana to the railhead at Kelton, Utah, was a four hundred mile journey through uninhabited country. The road agents would lie in wait at the narrow Port Neuf canyon, forty miles from old Fort Hall. There they captured treasure after treasure. The folklore of Idaho abounds in tales of such loot, hidden by fleeing bandits and never, to this day, recovered.

It was while driving through this canyon that Beidler and Clark were hailed by a band of Plummer's men. Both driver and treasure guard were armed and shot their way through the ambush. Later, they identified the robbers, who were killed by vigilantes, as were many other outlaw gangs of the West.

In the late 1870's, when Clark was a man of thirty-five or

183

thirty-six, he was riding guard on the stages that carried gold bullion from the great Homestake mine at Lead, South Dakota, to the railhead at Sydney, Nebraska. This coach was held up on almost every run, as it carried vast treasure. The largest shipment over this road was $350,000 worth of gold bullion in July of 1877, at the period when the activities of the road agents were most vicious.

No record had been found of a single successful hold up when Clark was riding as guard. He often rode with Boone May, also considered one of the most deadly shots on any road. The outlaws were never eager to exchange fire with these two famous men. By that time, the treasure chest had been made safer. It was now lined with lead and was too heavy to be easily "thrown down." Also, the treasure coaches had discontinued the practice of carrying passengers, except in emergencies. The shotgun guard was free to exchange bullets without the added danger of harming innocent passengers.

What happened to Clark Stocking, the youngest treasure guard, after the treasure coaches were discontinued is not known. When the railroads reached the mines, such jobs as Clark's were no longer needed. No town has been named for this brace youth who performed a valuable, but little known, service in the early West. No monument has been raised in his memory. However, as a young man he assumed and performed with distinction one of the most dangerous occupations of the period.

SUGGESTIONS FOR FURTHER READING

Of the hundreds of books dealing with the early West, the following may prove interesting for further reading about noted people who began their careers as teen-agers.

BISHOP, CURTIS. *Lone Star Leader: Sam Houston;* Julian Messner, 1961.

BLASSINGAME, WYATT. *Sacagawea, Indian Guide;* Garrard Publishing Co., 1965.

————. *Bent's Fort;* Garrard Publishing Co., 1967.

BURT, OLIVE W. *Camel Express;* Winston, 1954.

————. *Jayhawker Johnny;* The John Day Company, Inc., 1966.

————. *Mountain Men of the Early West;* Hawthorn Books, Inc., 1967.

————. *Petticoats West;* Julian Messner, 1962.

CROSBY, ALEXANDER L. *Steamboat up the Colorado;* Little, Brown and Co., 1965.

DUNN, J. P. *Massacres of the Mountains;* Archer House, out of print.

HAVIGHURST, WALTER. *Annie Oakley of the Wild West;* Macmillan Co., 1954.

KELLY, CHARLES. *Miles Goodyear;* Private printing, 1937.

LUCE, WILLARD & CELIA. *Jim Bridger;* Garrard Publishing Co., 1966.

NEUBERGER, RICHARD L. *The Lewis and Clark Expedition;* Random House, Inc., 1951.

PETERS, DEWITT C. *Kit Carson's Life and Adventures;* Dustin, Gilman, 1873.

RAYFORD, JULIAN LEE. *Child of the Snapping Turtle— Mike Fink;* Abelard-Schuman, 1951 Limited.

WHITE, DALE. *Fast Draw Tilghman;* Julian Messner, 1959.

INDEX

188

191